Janette Myers

dorothy grant hennings

smiles, nods, and pauses

activities to enrich children's communication skills

citation press/new york

To my sister Barbara

For reprint permission, grateful acknowledgment is made to:

Harcourt Brace Jovanovich, Inc. for "Wide Awake" by Myra Cohn Livingston from *Wide Awake and Other Poems*, © 1959 by Myra Cohn Livingston.

Harper & Row, Publishers for "Spring" by Karla Kuskin from *In the Middle of the Trees*, copyright © 1958 by Karla Kuskin.

The World Publishing Company for "One Old Ostrich" by Charles Francis Potter from *More Tongue Tanglers and a Rigmarole*, copyright © 1964 by Clara Cook Potter.

Photo credit, Marjorie Pickens

Published by Citation Press, Library and Trade Division,
Scholastic Magazines, Inc., Editorial office:
50 West 44th Street,
New York, New York 10036.

Library of Congress Catalog Card Number: 73-94479
International Standard Book Numbers:
0-590-7388-5 (Hardcover)
0-590-9580-3 (Paperback)
Second printing, 1976

CONTENTS

before beginning

This book is an exploration of nonverbal language—
    language that reaches out through silence
    to communicate meanings that words alone cannot
    convey.

This book is a source—
    a source of activities in which youngsters can
    express and interpret meanings with more than words.

This book is a beginning—
    a beginning from which teachers can venture on their
    own to develop nonverbal communication skills in
    boys and girls.

This book is a plea—
    a plea to teachers to build language arts programs
    that emphasize not just words.

A note of appreciation is due those who made it possible for me to write *Smiles, Nods, and Pauses*. The help of Alice Lawlor in locating relevant resource materials is sincerely appreciated as are the suggestions of my colleagues in English education at Kean College of New Jersey: Lillian Lemke, John Ramos, and Myra Weiger. Special thanks go also to Ruth Small, Administrative Assistant in the South Brunswick schools. To my husband, George, who read, reread, proofread, and supplied ideas and encouragement from beginning to end, I say a thank you that goes beyond words.

D.G.H.

I: say it with more than words

El Exigente is a familiar figure to most American TV viewers. Dressed in an impeccable white suit, head held high, body ramrod straight, face expressionless, he epitomizes the viewer's concept of a demanding one—one who expects and will accept only the best. In the now almost classic commercial, as El Exigente lifts cup to lips, a smile breaks across his impassive face, and the TV viewer knows that the demanding one has found and is enjoying the very best in coffee. When El Exigente speaks at the end of the commercial, his few words are almost extraneous. He has already said it all without words.

The Alka-Seltzer commercials of recent years also go beyond words to communicate their message to the viewer. Take, for instance, the commercial in which a man stands in front of a delicatessen showcase and describes his experience with stuffed peppers. Tone of voice and facial expressions make explicit the fact that he chose the peppers and is now suffering the consequence, an upset stomach. Adding to the effect is the face of the all-knowing clerk in the background whose expression clearly says, "I told you so!"

Messages conveyed with more than words are just as much a part of everyday life as they are of TV commercials. That this is true is verified by the work of a growing number of authorities in the newly developed field of kinesics—the scientific study of nonverbal communication—authorities such as Edward T. Hall, R. L. Birdwhistell, Erving Goffman, Albert E. Scheflen, Robert Sommer, and Paul Wachtel. That this is true can also be verified quite simply by an exercise in self-analysis. Think about the most

recent conference you held with a parent, and ask
yourself the following questions:

1. If you are male, did you slip into your jacket before
   the parent arrived? Knowing that you had a conference scheduled for that day, did you choose attire
   different from your everyday school dress? If so, why?
   If you are female, did you freshen your lipstick and
   comb your hair before the parent's arrival? Knowing
   that you had a conference scheduled for that day, did
   you specially select the outfit you wore? If so, why?
2. Before the parent arrived, did you make an attempt
   to straighten your desk, to put things in place, or to
   make the room slightly more attractive? If so, why?
3. Before the parent entered the room, did you have
   some notion about where you would hold the conference—at your desk, at a table, or at student desks?
4. At the parent's arrival, did you give him your immediate attention or did you ask him to wait while you
   completed a task?
5. When you settled down to talk, approximately how
   many feet separated the two of you? Did you at any
   time move closer to the parent? back off from the
   parent? change your position relative to the parent?
   touch the parent? Why?
6. During the conference was your tone of voice different from the tone of voice you tend to use with your
   students? at home with your family? in the teachers'
   room? If you answer yes, consider why you vary your
   tone of voice with different audiences.
7. How did the precision with which you spoke during
   the conference compare with your usual enunciation
   at home? in the teachers' room? in the principal's
   office?
8. How did the volume of your voice during the conference compare with your projection when you teach?
9. When you heard the parent's footsteps in the hall, did

you walk toward the door to greet him? Why? Why not?

10. How did you tell the parent where to sit?

11. How did you indicate to the parent that the conference was terminating and it was time to leave?

12. In what ways did you use your body to clarify a point you were making? For example, did you use your hands to describe something? pantomime with your body to show a behavior typical of the parent's child? use your fingers to count off items in a series? use your hands to make more explicit a contrast which you were making?

13. In what ways did you use your body to focus the parent's attention on something? For example, did you gesture toward the bulletin boards? a listening-speaking station? a work area? the reading corner? Did you point to particular items in the student's record or to a paper held in your hand?

14. In what ways did you use your hands, head, or body to emphasize a point you were making verbally?

15. During the conference did you ever feel yourself smiling or nodding almost deliberately?

16. Do you recall making eye contact with the parent as you conversed?

17. Do you recall receiving a nonverbal message from the parent during the conference? How did you respond?

18. Did you form any opinions about the parent based on his appearance? his tone of voice? his enunciation? the loudness with which he projected his voice? his posture? the way he made eye contact with you?

19. Did you ever have the feeling that he was deliberately using stance, tone of voice, gestures, or pauses to create a specific impression?

20. Did you notice any nonverbal signs indicating nervousness—fiddling with coins, tapping of fingers, jiggling of feet, or twisting of a ring? Were you exhibiting any of these types of nonverbal behavior?

HOW WE SAY IT WITH MORE THAN WORDS

Let's go back now and check your responses to the twenty questions in a rather informal way. In so doing, we will begin to identify components of nonverbal language and draw conclusions about how we communicate with more than words. These conclusions will be the conceptual base upon which classroom activities are designed to develop children's nonverbal language skills.

APPEARANCE On days when you anticipate parent conferences, you may very well select a form of attire slightly different from the garb you wear for classroom teaching. You may put on your Harris tweed jacket and wear your honor key tie clip. If you are female, you may substitute a newer dress for your everyday sweater suit and add one of your better pieces of jewelry. Then, too, just before the conference you probably put on your jacket or checked to see if your make-up is fresh.

Erving Goffman in *The Presentation of Self in Everyday Life* (Doubleday/Anchor, 1959, p. 24) classifies appearance as one component of the front that a person wittingly or unwittingly maintains before others and that defines a situation for other participants. Appearance, according to Goffman, tells others of one's social status, of one's view about the formality or informality of the occasion, of one's view about the importance of the occasion, and of one's view of self. In this respect, appearance carries significant communication impact.

THE SETTING Another part of the front people present to others is what Goffman (p. 24) terms setting—the "furniture, decor, physical layout, and other background items which supply the scenery and stage props for the spate of human action played out before, within, or upon it." When you have children construct attractive bulletin boards or make a special attempt to tidy up the room just before a siege of parent conferences, you are recognizing that setting speaks. You know—perhaps intuitively—that a classroom setting tells a visitor something about the teacher and about the kinds of learnings going on in his room.

The way you organize furniture for the conference speaks for you just as definitively as your appearance. Where you position yourself in relation to your visitor tells much. As the research evidence being compiled by Robert Sommer indicates (*Personal Space: The Behavioral Basis of Design,* Prentice-Hall, 1969, pp. 20–3), some seating arrangements carry a built-in message about the status of participants. Look, for instance, at these three conference patterns:

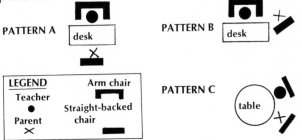

CONFERENCE PATTERNS THAT SEND DIFFERENT MESSAGES

In which situation is the teacher suggesting a dominant role for himself? In which is he suggesting a less structured conversation? In which will it be easiest to develop a more intimate discussion?

The kinds of furniture and the manner in which furniture is manipulated also define for participants their role in the situation. More simply stated, who gets the more comfortable chair says a lot! Who gets up and gives his more comfortable chair to someone else says even more about the status and the relationship of the people interacting. For this reason, setting—including furnishings, decor, and layout—is as integral a component of nonverbal language as is personal appearance.

TIME Another component of nonverbal language is time and the way it is handled. Discussing the significance of time in sending messages, the noted anthropologist Edward T. Hall (*The Silent Language*, Doubleday, 1959, p. 23) emphatically states: "Time talks. It speaks more plainly than words. The message it conveys comes through loud and clear. Because it is manipulated less consciously, it is subject to less distortion than the spoken language. It can shout the truth where words lie."

A few examples will clarify Hall's point. To Americans, keeping a person waiting for a conference while finishing up a paper-work task may suggest that the paper is more important than the person. Coming early to a conference may suggest high interest, concern, or even great respect for the conferee, whereas arriving late might well suggest just the opposite. Having two or more different conferences going on at the same time is considered "somewhat immoral," and a conferee who receives only intermittent attention from someone who is his equal and whom he has come to see by appointment may feel rebuffed.

Hall makes the point that the messages sent by time are cultural derivatives; in other words, people who have grown up in one culture draw inferences about time that may differ from inferences drawn by peoples of another cultural background. For example, whereas Americans attach considerable significance to keeping appointments, Iranians treat appointments with a lesser sense of commitment. The Sioux attach almost no significance to promptness; as Hall explains, the Sioux do not even have a word for time in their language. In contrast, the Japanese handle time with more exactness than Americans. This evidence leads to the conclusion that interpretation of nonverbal clues must be based on knowledge of the cultural background of an individual. To judge a message in terms of one's own cultural norms is to court misinterpretation—something that does occur when different cultures meet.

SPACE Space speaks too. When conversing with co-workers or acquaintances, adult Americans tend to keep four to seven feet of distance between them; they function within a space that Hall terms *close social distance* (Edward T. Hall's *The Hidden Dimension,* Doubleday, 1966, pp. 110–120). Moving closer than four feet implies a less formal, warmer relationship, for now people are functioning within *personal space*—a space reserved for chatting with friends. Moving nearer to about eighteen inches between brings one into another's *intimate space* that is reserved almost exclusively for loved ones, for children, and for people performing a service function. Strangers who move in this close tend to make the average American feel uncomfortable and wonder what is going on.

To move away, of course, sends the opposite kind of message from the one sent by moving together. Moving away may signal a desire to keep the relationship formal and impersonal. According to Hall, the distance between seven and twelve feet is commonly used in social or business relationships—it is still social distance but Hall calls this distance *far social* to suggest added remoteness. If you conduct parent conferences as shown in Pattern A, (see p. 5) you are probably putting seven feet as well as the barrier desk between yourself and the parent. You are implying through your use of space that yours is a rather formal relationship.

Very infrequently do people talk on a one-to-one basis with more than twelve feet intervening. Twelve feet and beyond is *public distance*; it is commonly used by lecturers who are addressing a group or by people who are approaching a public figure—the queen, the president, or the star. Interaction carried on at this distance is characterized by an even greater degree of formality than far social distance.

Touch is a way to cut across distance. Touch breaks through social and personal space and establishes a more intimate relationship. Touch is often used to assure, to console, to say "I understand, I care." In America, men generally refrain from touching other men. Women touch other women only after establishing themselves as friends. Men are careful about touching women with whom they do not have a close relationship. Women are a little freer to touch men with whom they do not have a personal relationship. Almost everyone feels free to touch a young child. Only in periods of extreme stress—at deaths, at traumatic moments—do these general prohibitions break down. In everyday encounters touch is not frequent among American adults. For that reason, touch speaks strongly.

VOCAL MANNER Goffman identifies *manner* as another element of the façade that people unwittingly or deliberately employ in interaction with others. Manner communicates the role a person expects to play in the interaction. Through his manner, a person may say that he expects to take a leadership role in the conversation; conversely his manner may say that he expects to follow the other's lead.

Tone of voice is a basic component of manner. Tone can be assertive, demanding, condescending, gentle, uncertain, unhappy, friendly, questioning, or pleasant. Likewise, loudness and rate of delivery can communicate self-control or lack of it, thoughtful consideration or a get-it-over-with attitude, timidity or dominance, excited interest or passive disinterest. Pitch of voice and variations in pitch have a similar communicative value. Speaking in a monotone may suggest boredom or tiredness, whereas varying pitch may communicate interest. Speaking in a squeaky, high voice may suggest nervousness; speaking in a low, unhurried voice may communicate control over the situation.

Very often vocal manner packs a greater punch

than the actual words used. The words spoken may be rather bland. Tone, loudness, pitch, and rate are what get attention and tell the listener "I am displeased!" or "I can't stand you!" or "I'm boss here!" or "You have done a fine job!"

There is little doubt that people can discriminate feelings expressed through vocal manner. Researchers have studied extensively the vocal expression of feelings. Their technique has been to have people read a verbal passage in several different ways, each time expressing a specific emotion. As Joel Davitz reports (*The Communication of Emotional Meaning,* McGraw-Hill, 1964, pp. 23–9), listeners to recordings have identified the feelings expressed to an extent greater than could have been accounted for just by chance. Based on this evidence, it seems safe to conclude that vocal manner is an inherent part of our language system. To communicate effectively, a person must be able to express and interpret vocal meanings.

BODY LANGUAGE Another aspect of manner is body language. Gestures, gross motions of the body, facial expressions, the way eye contact is maintained, posture—all these signal the role a participant is playing and expects to play in an interaction. For example, in a parent conference, if you go to the door to greet the parent, if you gesture toward a seat, if you pick up a file folder to signal the beginning of the serious discussion, and if you signal the end of the conference by standing up, you are assuming a leadership role by sending nonverbal clues that say "I am in charge here." In contrast, if you are entering a conference with your boss, you probably exhibit an entirely different set of nonverbal responses. You may cock your head to one side to ask, "Where do you want me to sit?" You may physically hold back until given a sign to enter, to sit, or to leave. Your way of holding your body may differ, too. No longer is your body saying "leader"; it may well be saying "submissive follower."

The language of the body, however, does more than establish the boundaries within which participants function. Body language sends messages that help to clarify meanings being discussed. While describing an object, a speaker may use his hands to show its shape, its size, or its location. When comparing or contrasting objects or ideas, a speaker gestures with one hand while describing one object, then gestures with his other hand when talking about a second object. Similarly, a speaker uses his hands to indicate steps in a sequence. A speaker points to show who, what, where, or to focus attention.

Body language that clarifies involves more than hands and arms. Motions of the feet can demonstrate how to perform a dance step. Motions of the torso can demonstrate rhythm. A walking-toward motion can tell who, what, or where. Looking-at can focus attention. And sometimes in normal conversation, motions of hands, arms, torso, legs, and eyes occur simultaneously as a speaker uses pantomime to communicate. A speaker *becomes* the tennis player making a serve; he stands up and with his whole body demonstrates the stroke. Or talking about a ride in a horse-drawn wagon down a bumpy country road, he lets his whole body go and pretends he is back in the cart bumping up and down, this way and that.

In addition, body language sends messages about the importance people attach to the words they speak. A pounding of the foot, a jabbing of the hand, a shaking of the head, a rapping on the desk, a slamming down of books can say that a speaker is really serious, excited, interested, or angry. His body statements add emphasis to his verbal statements. They help to express his feelings.

A vast range of feelings can be expressed physically—joy, fatigue, displeasure, distaste, anticipation, concern, nervousness, or restlessness. These emotions can be expressed on the face, told through the eyes, or shown through body stance, gestures, and actions. Julius Fast in *Body Language* (Pocket Books, 1971, p. 163) reports a study conducted by Norman Kagan of Michigan State University. In the Kagan study, deaf people were shown films in which technical problems made lip reading impossible. By focusing on body language, however, the men and women were able to interpret the emotional states of the filmed people. Words played no part in their interpretations.

A different kind of feeling sent nonverbally is physical discomfort triggered by environmental stimuli. First, there are the physical reactions to the natural environment. For example, a person shows his discomfort on a hot day by fanning motions, by wiping perspiration from his brow, by pulling a sticking shirt away from his hot body. He shows that direct sunlight in his eyes is bothersome by squinting, by shading his eyes with his hand, by hunching down to avoid the light, or by rubbing his eyes. Second, there are the nonverbal clues that indicate physical discomfort originating internally. The hand-to-nose to stop a sneeze, the blowing of the nose, or the momentary scratching of an itch are examples of such nonverbal clues. Then there are nonverbal clues that indicate a person is suffering discomfort from clothing. A loosening of the collar, a pulling at a tight waist band, the tucking in of a shirt that has popped out, the pulling up of a slip strap are cases in point—all signs that the person is trying to adjust to environmental conditions.

Still another kind of information can be transmitted nonverbally—lack of understanding and lack of attention. A look can say, "I don't understand." Eyes that gaze into space can say, "My mind is somewhere else." Clues such as these are important to a person who is trying to communicate. They supply a speaker with immediate feedback. They tell him whether he needs to re-explain, whether he is boring, or whether he is antagonizing his listener. In response to this feedback, the perceptive speaker modifies both the verbal and nonverbal statements he is making.

Body language—particularly the language of the eyes—performs yet another function in communication. Dr. Ralph Exline's work at the University of Delaware, Dr. Gerhard Nielson's work at the University of Copenhagen—both reported by Fast in *Body Language*—and the investigations of Dr. Kenneth Strongman of the University of Exeter, England, tell us that the eyes play almost a regulatory role in conversation. Looking away and pausing while speaking says, "I'm still talking. Please don't interrupt." Locking gaze and pausing while speaking says, "Now I'm finished. What do you think?" These physical maneuvers serve much the same function as the more complex process of raising hands and recognizing participants, typical of classroom interaction. Eye maneuvers are rather difficult to identify by recalling previous interactions. You may find it worthwhile to sit back and watch others as they converse to see just how the eyes regulate the verbal give-and-take.

SUMMARY To say it with more than words is to say it with appearance, with setting, with time, with space, with vocal manner, and with body language. Although words probably carry most of the cognitive meanings we send to one another, the ways we move and hold our bodies, the signals our eyes emit, the expressions on our faces, the tonal quality of our voices, the distances that we maintain between ourselves and others, the speed with which we react, and even the way we handle silence are as significant in determining whether we get our messages across as the actual words spoken. Likewise, our ability to perceive nonverbal clues and to use these clues to regulate conversation may determine whether we receive the full import of messages sent to us.

Writers of commercials such as the El Exigente coffee and the Alka-Seltzer sequences recognize the impact of messages sent with smiles and pauses. The commercials use nonverbal clues purposefully to build an effect and to make a more lasting impression than words alone can create. It is only in recent years, however, that there has been a widespread realization that nonverbal language is an integral part of everyday communication and that nonverbal clues can be used as purposefully to create an impression in everyday conversations as they are in the world of advertising.

WHY WE NEED TO TEACH CHILDREN NONVERBAL SKILLS

With realization of the importance of nonverbal clues in communication has come a parallel realization that a language program in schools is incomplete unless it includes meaningful encounters with nonverbal language. For people living in today's technologically oriented, fast-paced world, such encounters are vital. They are vital because:

- Nonverbal clues may be used as part of impression management, that is, the control of others' impressions of oneself,
- There is greater contact between diverse cultural groups—groups who may attach different meanings to a nonverbal signal.
- People need to become fully functioning human beings, able to express both verbally and nonverbally what they really are.

Each of these factors is considered at length in the following sections.

IMPRESSION MANAGEMENT   Masters of the art of persuasion are also masters of nonverbal language.

They bombard their audiences with many stimuli—stimuli that gain impact from shrewd manipulation of appearance, setting, timing, and spatial relationships as well as from vocal manner and body English. Persons naive about the intricacies of the fine art of "impression management," as Goffman calls it, are sitting ducks for every con artist or high-powered salesman who comes along.

In this technological age, a turn of the TV dial brings such high-powered salesmen directly into our homes. Making extensive use of nonverbal language, commercials convince men, women, and children to spend their money on things they really do not need and cannot afford.

Similarly, the face-to-face salesperson who expertly manages nonverbal and verbal language often can convince a customer to buy something totally unwanted, overpriced, or inferior in quality. The seller uses all the tricks of persuasion. He moves into the personal space of the customer, even placing a confiding hand on the arm of an unsuspecting individual. Nonverbally his actions say, "Look here, you are a friend of mine. I will let you in on a good deal that I don't give to everyone." He uses eye contact to suggest directness and integrity. He times his hard-sell attack, sensing through nonverbal signals when the potential customer is weakening. He may literally get a foot inside a customer's house to give a home demonstration. He knows that a person who accepts services may feel a commitment to buy.

Direct selling of products is not the only area of living in which impression management has been and is being employed. It is easy to identify similar deliberate use of nonverbal language to create positive impressions:

- Successful politicians are generally pros at impression management. They have to convince the voter that they have the voter's welfare in mind and that they are telling it the way it really is. They must come across as honest, warm, and approachable. They can hardly afford to appear too passive or a voter might question their capacity for decisive leadership; they must come across as strong and reliable.
- Actors and actresses use impression management to create a particular kind of public image, an image that may have its origins in the mind of some public relations man.
- Suitors, both male and female, use impression management to make a particular kind of impression upon a prospective mate, an impression that may not represent what they really are. This may be one factor accounting for later dissatisfaction with the marriage partner; after the honeymoon, the partner ceases to pretend, and the real self begins to surface.
- Individuals with low rank in the social pecking order may use impression management techniques to project images of themselves that conform with the image of excellence held by individuals of higher rank. For example, students may project an image that the teacher approves of, a teacher may project an image that the principal approves of, and an employee may project an image that meets the approval of his boss.

In short, impression management surrounds the average person in almost every phase of life—political, business, educational, and social. Thus, it is necessary for a person to be able to decipher the nonverbal messages he is receiving. It is necessary to be able to sift the underlying from the obvious messages sent deliberately by nonverbal language. And it is even more necessary to be able to use nonverbal language to send messages that say what one intends.

CULTURAL DIVERSITY As has been mentioned previously, all cultures do not draw upon an identical nonverbal vocabulary. Time, space, and touch are viewed differently by people of diverse cultures. What is considered normal distance for social contact by one group may be considered close by another; what is considered as late by one group may be on-time for others.

The same can be said of gestures and overall manner. A particular way a man looks at a woman may be considered rude by one group; women of a different culture may feel rebuffed if they are not looked at in that way. A particular manner may be considered tremendously overbearing by one group; a person in another culture may have no chance for success unless he behaves in that manner.

Because of these differences, a person crossing cultures runs the risk of offending others unless he promptly sets for himself the task of understanding the nonverbal language of the other group. In a period of rapid transportation and numerous cross-cultural encounters, the need for heightened awareness of the import of nonverbal communication and for the skills to analyze the vocabulary of nonverbal language is obvious.

ABILITY TO EXPRESS Julius Fast, the writer who has done so much to popularize the concept of body language, describes the experiences of a very beautiful teen-age girl at a dance who stood "near the wall with a girl friend, haughty, aloof and unapproachable, for all the world like the snow maiden in the fairy tale." When asked why she held herself so aloof, she answered:

I was distant? . . . What about the boys? Not one of them came up and talked to me. I was dying to dance but no one asked me. . . . I'm the only teen-age old maid in school. Look at Ruth. She's my age and she danced every dance, and you know her. She's a mess. (*Body Language,* Pocket Books, 1971, p. 171)

But as Fast points out, Ruth—though a "mess"—knew how to cut through a boy's defenses; her body language said "yes." In contrast, the cool "snow maiden" unconsciously was signaling, "No, do not approach; I don't want you." Fast asks, "What teenage boy will take a chance at such a rejection?" He goes on to suggest that with practice the unapproachable young lady

may learn to smile and soften her beauty and make it attainable. She'll learn the body language to signal boys, "I can be asked, and I'll say yes." But first she must understand the signals. She must see herself as she appears to others, she must confront herself and only then can she change.
   All of us can learn that if we express the *we* that we want to be, the *we* that we are hiding, that we can make ourselves more available and free ourselves (p. 171).

It is Fast's conclusion that to express our real selves we must understand the signals. His conclusion sums up for this writer why teachers must help children to say it with more than words. Life is an adventure to be lived fully. To live fully, each individual needs the skills to express what he is without inhibition and with an understanding of the meanings his messages send. An individual needs to know how to reach out to others, to say yes and even no with the whole of his being, to speak with all the power of language—verbal and nonverbal—that he can command. He needs to perceive the impact of his messages on others and adjust his messages to meet the uniqueness of a situation. He must come to accept his own body—the shape of it, the size of it, and the look of it. He must appreciate the capacity of his body to express meanings and feel free to express himself using arms, eyes, legs, fingers; feet, face, or torso.

HOW TO TEACH CHILDREN TO COMMUNICATE WITH MORE THAN WORDS

The way to achieve this educational task is *not* to teach children how to "plant" or "drop" specific gestures into a conversation, or how to "paint" particular expressions on the face, or how to cover up feelings with a nonverbal mask. Such techniques only scratch the surface superficially; they fail to take into account the wholeness of human behavior and interject a phoniness into interaction.

A more comprehensive approach is called for—one based on totally involving children in the "vocabulary" of expression. Encounters with people, with ideas, with stories, and with things that encourage free and uninhibited expression can be built into the curriculum. Particularly appropriate are activities that stimulate pantomiming and dramatic behavior, discussions that require both verbal and nonverbal expression, storytelling experiences that force a child or youth to communicate with all the powers he can command, and movement experiences that free inhibitions and muscles and allow a child to "do his thing." Interpretive experiences through which a child or youth listens not just to words but to nonverbal language are important in the curriculum, too.

Incorporating the development of nonverbal skills into a comprehensive program in the communication arts is the major premise upon which this volume is based. The following chapters describe specific ideas for encounters with nonverbal language. The activities in each section become progressively more difficult so that, in general, those at the beginning are most suitable for younger children, and those at the end can be handled by upper-grade students.

But before teachers can help children handle nonverbal language, we must begin with ourselves. We may feel inhibited in expressing meanings with our bodies. We may find that we have not been using the communication impact inherent in appearance, setting, space, and time as part of our message, or we may not have been consciously listening for nonverbal feedback.

If that is true, when we teach children nonverbal language skills, we teach ourselves simultaneously. We do this by at times playing the silent observer and analyzing consciously the nonverbal signals of others. An observation guide such as the following can make the task easier. We also learn by participating actively in classroom pantomiming, role playing, storytelling, and dramatizing, and by moving about with children as they play action games. Rather than acting simply as director, we too can relax and fly to the accompaniment of "Ebb Tide." We can pretend we are grasshoppers and be part of a grasshopper chain with children. We can play the role of the mean witch or the fairy godmother and improvise words and actions even as youngsters do. And when we teach, we can move from behind our desks and from behind the wall of our own inhibitions to reach out to children and free our bodies to express what we really feel.

AN OBSERVATION GUIDE FOR TEACHERS TO USE IN STUDYING NONVERBAL MESSAGES

1. APPEARANCE

What specific messages are being sent:

Through the clothing of participants in the situation?

Through the hair styling of participants?

Through the apparent state of health and cleanliness of participants?

Through the makeup and jewelry of participants?

What verbal and nonverbal clues lead to the impression that participants are:

Deliberately using aspects of appearance to create an effect?

Aware of the impression being created by another's appearance?

2. SETTING

What specific messages are being sent:

By the general décor?
By the kind of furniture?
By the arrangement of furniture?
By the background items?
By the use of light, shadow, and darkness?
By the use of color?
By the temperature?

What verbal and nonverbal clues lead to the impression that a participant is:
Deliberately using aspects of setting to create an effect?
Aware of messages sent via setting?

3. TIME
What specific messages are being sent:
By participants' organization of time?
By participants' awareness of time obligations?

What clues are there suggesting a deliberate use of time to communicate a message?

4. SPACE
What specific messages are being communicated:
By the physical space maintained between participants?
By changes of distance between participants?
By the physical contact (touching) that occurs between participants?

What clues suggest a deliberate use of distance and touch to communicate?

5. VOCAL MANNER
What specific messages are being communicated vocally:
Through tone of voice?
Through rate of delivery?
Through loudness of delivery?

Through pitch?
Through periods of silence?

What clues suggest a deliberate use of voice to communicate?

What clues suggest that a participant received a message sent vocally?

6. BODY LANGUAGE

What physical signals define the roles of participants in the situation?

What specific cognitive meanings are communicated physically:
Through gestures?
Through facial expressions?
Through gross body motions such as walking, running, pacing?
Through expressions of the eyes?
Through body stance?
Through pantomiming motions of the entire body?

What specific emotional meanings are communicated physically:
Through gestures?
Through facial expressions?
Through gross body motions such as walking, pacing, running?
Through expressions of the eyes?
Through body stance?
Through expressive motions of the entire body?

What specific nonverbal clues suggest that a participant is reacting to discomfort or comfort triggered:
By the immediate external environment?
By his own bodily condition?
By aspects of his attire?

What evidence is there that a participant in the conversation is reacting to the body language feedback of listeners?

How do participants signal one another that they:
Are listening?
Are pausing momentarily but want to continue to speak?
Are pausing to give another a chance to speak?
Agree with a speaker?
Disagree with a speaker?

11: ACTIONS SPEAK LOUDER THAN WORDS

One of the easiest and perhaps most enjoyable type of activity through which children and youths can encounter the basic elements of body language is pantomime. In pantomime the entire message is conveyed physically through facial expression, eye movement, body stance, speed of activity, motions of the total body, and gestures of hands, head, arms, feet, torso, and legs. School children can play with pantomiming in many ways: they can express with body language the meanings suggested by words and sentences; they can simulate the shape and movement of objects with their bodies; they can tell a story without using spoken words. In addition they can play games in which the total action is conducted nonverbally; participants are indicated, reactions made, and responses given through gestures and facial expressions.

The purpose of including pantomime-play activities in the school curriculum is three-fold. First, pantomiming can help a child or youth feel more free and less inhibited in expressing ideas and feelings through body language. An individual may feel uncomfortable when expressing himself nonverbally; he is not at ease with his own body and as a result is unable to use his body as an effective communication agent. For this youngster, pantomime is a way of loosening muscles and releasing inhibitions so that nonverbal expression becomes a natural part of his everyday communication repertoire.

A second purpose is heightened awareness of the communication impact of body language. By being forced to transmit his ideas and feelings completely without words and to receive and interpret messages being sent nonverbally by fellow-students, a youngster may begin to sense the importance of nonverbal clues in communication and to focus on more than words when he is listening to messages directed to him.

A third purpose of pantomime-play activity is development of skill in communicating nonverbally. Just as a youngster can build up facility in using verbal language, he can build up a facility in using his body to communicate. Through pantomiming, he can acquire the "vocabulary" of body language and gain skill in both sending and receiving nonverbal messages.

Of course, when a youngster is first asked to express an idea or feeling nonverbally as part of a pantomiming experience, he may not know where or how to begin; he is a prisoner of both his inhibitions and his lack of skill. Therefore, it is probably best to start with simple experiences in which participants communicate nonverbally the meaning implicit in one word or use their bodies to simulate concrete objects and explicit motions. Such simple activities build both skill and confidence and lay the foundation for more complex pantomime-play in which the total action and feelings of a story are told nonverbally.

Then, too, some preliminary loosening-up activities may be necessary to get children physically ready for pantomime. Before moving into an actual pantomime activity, children can stand up and "roll" the muscles of their backs, hang their heads and arms forward and swing "loose," or just swing their arms and legs in rhythm. Movement activities such as these help children to free both their muscles and inhibitions and provide a transition between verbal and body language.

PANTOMIMING WORDS

WALKING WITH FEELING   Play a recording of the song "Walking Happy," and have the children talk about how they walk when they are "walking happy" and how they walk when they are "walking sad." To a recording of "Happy Talk" from *South Pacific* have the children walk to express their feelings when they're happy. Then change to a recording of "Volga Boatman," and have the children walk to express their feelings when they are sad.

ACTION-WORD CHARADES   Divide the class into a number of small groups. Distribute to each group a card on which an action word such as rushed, crept, hobbled, strolled, marched, collapsed, crawled, sneaked, or pushed has been printed.

Write the sentence "The poor man _____ into the room." on the board. In their groups the students discuss briefly how to act out the sentence with the verb on their card placed in the blank. Then one person from a group acts out the sentence physically. From his actions, the other students try to guess the word. If the class cannot guess, a second youngster from the group tries to act out the word. If the class still cannot guess, another child from the group tries. When the word has been identified, the next group takes its turn.

With younger children, simplify the game by having the children act out more familiar words as in the following action-word sentence:

The little girl _____down the street.

skipped	walked	looked
hopped	ran	hurried
jumped	jumped rope	tiptoed

With older youngsters, more difficult words can be acted out and guessed. The following are suggested for the middle grades:

sauntered	stalked	strutted
sidled	flounced	cringed
catapulted	clattered	strode
hurtled	swaggered	ambled

Still other action words that can be pantomimed include:

hit	erase	stoop
picket	slap	stir
stretch	pat	glide
roll	tug	yawn
rub	throw	wink

After youngsters have played action-word charades several times with word cards prepared by the teacher, encourage pupil teams to find six or seven more action words, print the words on cards, and lead a future game. A thesaurus or a dictionary of synonyms can be helpful in locating words to be pantomimed. Pupil teams can look up words such as run, hurry, or fall in the Scott Foresman thesaurus *In Other Words,* locating synonyms for classroom groups to communicate physically.

FEELING-WORD CHARADES   Make individual feeling-word cards printed with such words as anxious, confused, tired, pleased, excited, unhappy, bored, and interested.

Divide the class into small groups; distribute a word card to each group. All members of a group simultaneously use body motions and facial expressions to communicate the feeling to other members of the class who must guess the feeling being expressed.

After all the groups have had a turn to express a feeling-word physically, collect the cards and redistribute them—again, one to a group. Now each group must express the feeling using only facial expressions. Again, the other children guess the word being expressed.

GRAB BAG RHYMING CHARADES   On cards print words such as:

fun	oat	toad
say	mat	face
take	house	pit
know	owl	tight
trick	rug	cease
live	lie	rain
see	ill	head
gave	can	care
flip	clock	bag

There should be a card for each member of the class.

Put all the cards into a large paper bag on which has been printed "Grab Bag Pantomime." Divide the class into three teams. A team member must come up front, pull a word card from the grab bag, look at it, think of a word that rhymes with the printed word (e.g. fun/run; say/lay; trick/pick), and pantomime the rhyming word. His fellow team members guess the word he is expressing nonverbally. If within two minutes, a team member guesses correctly, the team receives a point, and the card is put aside. If the team cannot guess, the card is returned to the bag, and the next team takes a turn.

When playing grab bag rhyming charades with young children, the word card can be shown to team members to make the guessing easier. With older children, understanding must come solely from the pantomimist's physical expressions.

PANTOMIMING SHAPES

BUILDING LETTERS Divide the class into groups of three or four. Give each group a letter of the alphabet printed on a card; good letters to use include v, o, i, t, x, l, s, n, and m.

Allow time for the groups to meet to determine how they physically can form the letter independently or through group action. Each group in turn presents its physical interpretation of the letter it received; the other class members guess the letter.

Sometimes it is fun for one group member to tell the guessers whether they are right or wrong by signalling nonverbally by shaking and nodding the head.

BUILDING SHAPES For this activity the class again

is divided into small groups. Each group receives a shape card on which is printed a word such as:

chair	table	elephant
airplane	tree	giraffe
tent	ball	bowl

Again allow time for the groups to meet to determine how they physically can form the shape either independently or cooperatively. One rule of this game is that players must build the shape without continued motion; once they have gotten into position—a position that communicates the shape—they must make their bodies rigid. Then, the others guess.

After the class has played with building shapes and letters, encourage them during seatwork activity periods to meet together in their shape groups to select a shape or letter to show bodily and to prepare the shape for class guessing. Put aside a few minutes at the end of the day for any shape groups (or motion groups) to do "their thing."

SHADOW PLAY Read to young children Beatrix Potter's classic *The Story of Peter Rabbit*. After reading, ask the children how they think Peter Rabbit ran when he was being chased by Mr. McGregor. When children volunteer to demonstrate, flash the light beam from a filmstrip projector on a screen or board, and ask the volunteers to cast their shadows on it. Dimming the lights makes the effect more striking.

Don't rush the fun; many children can become Peter Rabbit and show rabbit motion through their shadows.

After children have used their entire bodies to

simulate rabbit motion, suggest that they use only their hands to build Peter Rabbit's shape as a shadow. Then the projectionist flashes the light on black construction paper mounted on a bulletin board. When a child builds a rabbit-like shape with his hands, he maintains that position while another child traces with white chalk the outline of the rabbit's shadow onto the black paper. The projectionist then moves the light to another area of the black-covered bulletin board. Another child builds a rabbit shadow with his hands, which is in turn traced with white chalk by someone else. Each child who wants to project a rabbit can do so.

In independent work sessions during the following week, children can write about Peter Rabbit. Later they can print with chalk the words of their Peter story or poem inside or next to their rabbit outlines on the bulletin board.

Note: A similar activity can be carried out with such animals as flying horses, butterflies, birds, octopi, fish, and monsters.

NONVERBAL DESCRIPTIONS Write words or phrases that suggest a concrete image on large cards:

sphere	spiral staircase	on tiptoe
doughnut	big hole	waves crashing
small	immense	square
headfirst	up high	around
down	step by step	myself
you	here	there

Hold up the cards, one at a time. Students who want to express the meaning of these words and phrases through gestures show their interest by some nonverbal signal. Indicate which student is to do the pantomime by pointing or by using some other physical signal. Individually students pantomime the word or phrase; several students in turn can express the same word to show that there are often many gestures that can be used to send the same message.

KEEP WITHIN THE FRAME   Judith Humienik, a teacher of fifth-grade youngsters, has found that a large-framed area drawn on the chalk board can serve as a stage for pantomiming activity. The outlined frame is large enough to provide space for three or four youngsters to express a word, a shape, a feeling, or even a complicated sequence of actions. When one or more youngsters want to pantomime, they go to the area outlined on the board, and their actions become a moving picture within the frame.

PANTOMIMING MOTIONS

LET'S BE ANDY   Eleanor Schick has written a little book called *Andy* (Macmillan, 1971) that can be used in kindergarten or first grade to stimulate nonverbal expression. In the book everyone—Jamie, Wendy, and Joan—is too busy to play with Andy, so he plays by himself pretending to be, among other things, a workman riding a tractor and a cowboy herding cattle.

Children can nonverbally describe how Andy pretended to be the workman, the cowboy, and the other individuals in the story. Then they can nonverbally tell of things and people they pretend to be when they have no friends to play with.

Under Christopher's Hat by Dorothy M. Callahan (Scribners, 1972) has similar potential for stimulating nonverbal expression. Christopher, too, imagines that he is someone other than himself and role plays his imaginings.

THE WORK GAME Children can portray nonverbally the activity of different workers: farmer, traffic cop, moving man, doctor, teacher, typist, sweeper, truck driver, and the like.

In this game, the teacher can begin by acting out the movements of a worker. Then he calls nonverbally on a child who has indicated nonverbally that he wants to guess who the worker is. The guesser comes to the board and writes his guess there. The teacher reacts by shaking or nodding his head. If the guesser is wrong, another child is selected to write his guess on the board.

The student who guesses correctly becomes the next pantomimist, deciding for himself what worker he wants to portray. Again the guessing, reacting, and responding are done without spoken words.

MACHINE PLAY As a group activity children can simulate the action of machines with their bodies. They can pretend, for example, to be clocks or typewriters. Let them listen to a recording of Leroy Anderson's "The Syncopated Clock" and then in unison become clocks ticking with their bodies. Similarly, Anderson's "The Typewriter Song" can form a musical accompaniment for becoming typewriters or for pretending to type. In both activities children can make noises with their mouths to create sound effects to accompany their actions.

MORE MACHINE PLAY   Children stand in a line and create with their bodies the motion of a pneumatic drill; they can create vocal sound effects to accompany their actions. When each child has become a skilled pneumatic drill, have the child at the front of the line begin the action. The next child in line counts to himself, "1, 2, 3, 4, 5," and then he starts up his drill; as soon as the third child sees the second child begin the action, he counts to five, and begins. Each child in the line does the same until all the children are in motion. When the last child starts to move, he counts to ten, then taps the child before him on the shoulder, and stops moving. As soon as the child in front feels the tap, he stops moving and taps the child in front of him. In this way the beginning and the halting of motion are passed up and down the line in chain-reaction fashion.

On other occasions children can simulate the motions of trains, egg beaters, or bulldozers and send that motion down a line in similar chain-reaction fashion.

ANIMAL CHAINS   Children stand in a circle facing toward the center. First the children simulate in unison the motion of a snake with their bodies. When the children have begun to feel "snake-like," they all stop moving and hold their bodies motionless. Then the teacher points to one child who must begin to move like a snake. As soon as that child begins, the child on his right counts to five and then begins; as soon as he begins, the next child on his right counts to five and starts to move, and so on around the circle. When the motion gets back to the originating child, he counts to five and then stops, making his body completely motionless—and so on around the circle until all children have halted their action.

Children can carry on a similar pantomiming activity simulating other animal motions. On another day they can be horses trotting or grasshoppers jumping or birds gliding or even lobsters crawling on the ocean bottom. Let the children decide and concoct new kinds of motions to simulate physically.

Note: This activity has the added bonus that it forces children to be observant of the motion of other children, if the class is to really project a chain-reaction effect.

LET'S CLIMB ABOARD AND GO FOR A RIDE

Read aloud any of the many books available that tell a story about some kind of ride. Follow it up with a let's pretend riding activity. Children can pretend to be riding:

> In a wagon on a bumpy road,
> In Santa's sleigh,
> On a merry-go-round horse,
> In a car careening around corners at 80 mph,
> On a ship that's rocking,
> On a bicycle on a winding road.

Ask the children if they can think of other riding activities that they can all try out.

POPCORN

Bring an electric popcorn cooker and some corn to class. Children enjoy a corn popping experience and can watch the corn pop through the plastic or glass dome of the cooker. Talk about the motion. Share the corn. Then play a recording of "Popcorn" by Hot Butter; children can pretend they are corn bouncing up and down, getting ready to pop, and finally popping open.

A written activity can be a follow-up in which children write about corn popping, the taste of popcorn, or the way to make popcorn.

ORCHESTRAL PANTOMIME   If children attend a performance of the school orchestra, groups of children can concentrate on the activity of specific players. For example, some children can focus on the action of the trombonists, some watch the violinists, others study the celloists, while still others concentrate on the conductor. When the students return to the classroom, members of each group demonstrate pantomime-style how the instrument they observed is played.

A fun follow-up is to "perform" an orchestral selection as a class. To the accompaniment of a musical recording, all the players pantomime their parts in the orchestra as one member of the class "conducts." Run through a selection several times so that the youngsters begin to operate as a team and the different orchestral sections come in at the direction of the conductor.

Afterwards talk about times when people might use pantomime activity of this type as part of their natural conversation. Try to draw from the children the notion that if a person were describing how an instrument or machine works, he might include a nonverbal explanation as part of his description.

AUTUMN ACTION   On a crisp autumn day when leaves are beginning to fall, the class can take off for an excursion in nature. Walk through leaves with big kicking motions, throw leaves high in the air, and rake a big pile together. Then as children stand bundled together, read a little poetry piece such as:

RUN. . . . JUMP. . . . FALL
upon a pyramid
of leaping, swirling leaves;
smell their sharpness; feel their freshness;
brown and brittle; crisp and crunchy;
newly raked.

And children can jump into the pile, rake it up again, and jump once more.

When children have experienced this autumn action to its fullest, they can return to their classroom for talk and pantomime activity. Encourage them to talk about and describe what they did. Ask the children to show:

How we kicked leaves as we walked through them.
How we threw leaves into the air.
How we raked leaves into big piles.
How we jumped into the piles and
caused the leaves to fly.

Then the children can imagine what it is like to be a leaf falling from a high branch. The children close their eyes, hold their hands high above their heads, and pretend their hands are leaves floating downward.

Follow up this activity with written expression as children react to autumn action through story, description, and poetry.

PRE-PANTOMIME PLAY: CLIMBING A SPIRAL STAIRCASE Before involving children in complex pantomiming situations, do some preliminary play with simple situations in which every child in the class can participate. Climbing a spiral staircase is an example. Several children demonstrate climbing up a spiral staircase. Talk with the children about motions that could be interjected into an expressive sequence to communicate climbing upward; children may suggest leaning on the hand rail or raising the knees high or making jerking, sideward motions with the arms. As children suggest, of course, they demonstrate as well. Then all the children stand up and "climb a spiral staircase."

When the class has tried different ways of expressing the climbing action, the children can talk about and demonstrate how they would climb after climbing ten stories, twenty stories, or thirty stories. When they have some notion of actions to include, e.g. puffing, breathing heavily, leaning over, dragging the feet, pulling oneself up by the hand rail, begin THE CLIMB. After a minute or two of climbing, have a child leader call out, "We've reached the tenth floor!" After another minute or two of climbing, the leader calls out, "We've reached the twentieth floor!" After another minute or two, he announces, "We've reached the thirtieth floor!" Of course, at each stage of the climb, participants must adapt their style of climbing to the state of exhaustion they would feel. A climb such as this can be fun. It's an activity children enjoy repeating, so don't be afraid of coming back to it on another day.

Similar pre-pantomime play can center on the following situations:

• Pushing a heavy box across the floor and then pushing it up a hill.

- Walking a log stretched high across a brook.
- Lifting a weight that is light and then a weight that is extremely heavy.
- Stepping up to the plate to bat and then batting a strike, a ball, a foul ball, and finally a home run.

In each case, youngsters first talk about and then try out many possible actions before putting together a sequence of motions to express the total activity. All the youngsters can participate as they try out motions being discussed.

SOARING—LET'S PRETEND   Prepare a dittoed assignment sheet similar to this one:

```
THINK!                          G   IN THE
                                N
                                I           SKY
                                R
                                A           AIR
                                O
                                S           WIND
    THINK              G AND
         A             N                     CLOUDS.
         B             I
         O             Y
         U             L
         T             F
         SEAGULLS

ON TUESDAY, WE ARE GOING TO BECOME SEAGULLS.

BRING SOMETHING TO CLASS ON TUESDAY

         THAT
         WILL
         HELP YOU BECOME
                    A SEAGULL.
```

When the children arrive on Tuesday, read them portions of Richard Bach's *Jonathan Livingston Seagull* (Macmillan, 1972) that describe the plunging, soaring motions of gulls. Then the children don the things they have brought in to become seagulls. Darken the room slightly, push back the desks, and put on a recording of "Ebb Tide." The children become seagulls! Stress that they are not to pretend they are seagulls, but they must actually feel seagullish and believe they are seagulls.

This type of activity can also lead to verbal expression in the form of poetry writing.

ABC poetry works well in this context. Divide the class into six brainstorming groups. Each group gets one letter of the word *seagull*. The group thinks of words starting with the letter assigned that are associated with seagulls and lists as many words as it can on a portion of the chalkboard. The s–group, for instance, may think of soaring, sea, sun, sand, surf, sailing, sandy, sunny, sunshine, shiny, and shimmer. Encourage children to look in a dictionary for more words. When each group has compiled a sizeable listing, write the word *seagulls* across the board and then downward as shown below:

SEAGULLS

S

E

A

G

U

L

L

Seagulls.

Using the words that have been compiled else-
where on the board, children in groups (or as a
cooperative class activity) write a poem that describes how seagulls fly. The first line begins with an
s-word, the second line with an e-word, and so forth.
Remember that in this type of poetry, rhyming is
unnecessary; the ultimate goal is to express the feeling of being a seagull and to describe that feeling in
words that soar and fly.

WITCHES AND GOBLINS ON HALLOWEEN If the
children have shown enthusiasm for the "Soaring—
Let's Pretend" activity, try a similar experience. As
Halloween draws near, prepare another creative assignment sheet:

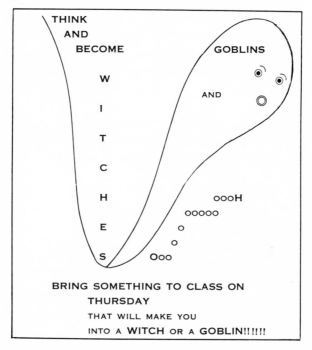

On Thursday push back the desks. As the children don their witch or goblin attire, darken the room. Play Moussorgsky's *A Night on Bald Mountain* for background accompaniment as the children become witches and goblins out for a night on Bald Mountain. This can be a vocal experience as well; children can whoop and howl like witches and goblins.

Keep an experience story chart ready on an easel. When youngsters have done their witches and goblins "thing," cluster them on the floor before the easel. Print the word *Witches* on the top line of the chart and ask the children to call out "ing" words that tell what witches do. They will give such words as howling, haunting, flying, swooping, and soaring. Ask them to select any two words that together have four syllables; these words become the second line of the poem. Ask where the witches haunt and suggest they try to tell in six syllables; these words become the third line of the poem. Then encourage the children to put together eight more syllables about witches to become the fourth line. The last line can simply be the word *witches* repeated. The result, of course, will be a cinquain—five lines of poetic expression with two, four, six, eight, and two as the syllable pattern for the lines.

Divide the class into three-person poetry writing teams. Each team is given a large piece of paper and records *goblins* as the first line. Repeating what they did as a class, the teams build cinquains. Suggest that as they think about goblins, they should "feel" goblinish and try out goblin movements before writing words on their paper. They should make a first draft on scrap paper and then rewrite their poems for sharing with the entire class.

OATMEAL FACE Jack Guilford, the well-known actor and mimic, performs a sensational act in which he moves his cheeks and eyes to simulate oatmeal boiling in a pot. Suggest to children that they try to make an "oatmeal face" at home by practicing before a mirror. Any child who thinks he knows how can try to make an "oatmeal face" before the class.

HAND SIGNALS A recording of R. Alex Anderson's "Lovely Hula Hands" can motivate discussion of the meanings that are sent through hand signals. Students listen to the words of the song, and, if they desire, they improvise hand motions as they listen a second time. Follow up with small group discussions in which boys and girls identify and list hand signals used in our society.

INDIAN SIGN LANGUAGE Children can have fun learning and expressing themselves through Indian sign language. Aline Amon's *Talking Hands: Indian Sign Language* (Doubleday, 1968) shows some of the hand signals that are part of Indian sign language. Reading that book can be a springboard to a discussion of the kinds of messages sent by hands and to actual communication based on the hand signals described in the book. If children want to, they can go on to invent their own secret system of sign language.

GIANT STEPS Giant steps is a game that can be played nonverbally. Players stand in a line facing the leader who is about twenty-four feet from the players. When played as a verbal game, the leader tells each player in turn, "You may take two (one, three, four, etc.) giant steps (or baby steps, jumping steps, hops, running steps, spins). Before obeying the player must ask, "May I?" The leader responds with "Yes, you may," in which case the player can make the move, or with "No, you may not," in which case the leader gives another command. If at any time the player fails to ask "May I?", he must return to the starting line. The first player to reach the finish line becomes the new leader.

To play the game nonverbally, translate the steps into a nonverbal code. For example, a giant step is indicated by holding the hands two feet apart, a baby step by holding the fingers close together, a hop by hopping the fingers. Now using the pre-established code, the leader gives his orders nonverbally. Players must extend their arms in a "May I?" gesture before obeying the order. If players fail to do this, they must go back to the starting line. If players fail to interpret the nonverbal command according to the pre-established code, they must also return to the starting line. This game is a good follow-up to work with Indian sign language, because to play it youngsters must invent their own nonverbal language.

PANTOMIMING SITUATIONS

REAL / UNREAL / HUMOROUS Youngsters can get the feel of some forms of real physical activity by actually performing the motions using the necessary equipment, e.g., playing catch using a regular ball. Encourage youngsters during this phase of the experience to become aware of and to focus on how they move their arms, feet, hands, mouths, shoulders, and so forth.

Next move to the *unreal* phase of the experience in which youngsters perform the physical motions without the real equipment, e.g., playing catch without a ball. This, of course, is a simulation experience. Real and simulation activities that are fun to try—some individually and some with others—include:

> Chewing and blowing bubble gum
> Playing jacks
> Brushing one's teeth
> Erasing and washing boards
> Playing Ping-pong
> Peeling a banana and eating it
> Taking off tight-fitting boots
> Cracking and eating a nut
> Sucking an all-day sucker
> Playing marbles
> Sweeping the floor
> Combing and grooming one's hair
> Threading a needle

When children "get the hang" of doing the unreal with about as much ease as they do the real, they often think about how they could add something *humorous* to their unreal activities. For instance, the bubble gum bubble bursts in one's face, the toothpaste turns out to be hand cream, or the all-day sucker falls and gets covered with dust that must be picked off speck by speck. Encourage creative children to add such humor to the unreal phase of their activities.

PETER AND THE WOLF *Peter and the Wolf* by

Prokofiev rates as a classic for stimulating nonverbal expression in classrooms. Play the record several times and listen for the key performers—the bird, the duck, the cat, the wolf, grandfather, and the hunters. Children can decide how each key part can be performed nonverbally to harmonize with the music and to communicate the characteristic physical activity. They try out suggested motions until they agree which motions "fit" each role.

The class divides into groups such as the hunters, grandfathers, and ducks. As children hear the appropriate melody indicating their part, they physically imitate the person or animal suggested and perform the predetermined motions.

The motions in this activity will have a staged appearance, since they have all been predetermined. However, because the activity is one in which the primary goal is to help children feel comfortable with nonverbal activity and not to produce an extravaganza performance for an audience, the fact that the motions are staged is not very significant.

THE SORCERER'S APPRENTICE   In the film *The Sorcerer's Apprentice* (Weston Woods), artist Lisl Weil draws to the musical accompaniment of the symphonic classic by Paul Dukas. Using broad strokes that involve her whole body, Ms. Weil fills a board with figures that make the music come alive.

After the class has viewed the film, mount large construction or mural paper on the wall and let the children try their hands at a musical mood interpretation of *The Sorcerer's Apprentice*. On other occasions children can interpret visually such pieces as:

Merideth Willson's "Seventy-six Trombones"
Peter Tchaikovsky's *Nutcracker Suite*
Richard Rodger's *The Sound of Music*
Albert Ketelbey's "In a Chinese Temple Gar-
    den," "In the Mystic Land of Egypt," "Jungle
    Drums," or "In a Persian Market."

In this activity, of course, the process of drawing
is more important than the pictures produced. Children working on large areas make circles, lines, and
shapes using large motions of their bodies; their
actions as well as their pictures interpret the musical
selection. Incidentally, *Ed Emberley's Drawing Book:
Make a World* (Little, Brown, 1972) is a fine book
that gives children ideas on how to represent the
world in a creative fashion. Emberley shows how to
create horses, skunks, seals, and other things through
a combination of simple lines and circles.

LET'S TELL A STORY   Read a story that involves
physical activity or the nonverbal expression of emotions. For instance, Ezra Jack Keats' *The Snowy Day*
(Viking, 1962) creates a feeling about snow through
the physical activities of Peter as he encounters the
soft, fluffy flakes. Peter makes angel prints in the
snow, slides down a hillside, and makes a snowball
to keep for always. In Edna Preston's *The Temper
Tantrum Book* (Viking, 1969), the lion, the elephant,
and the pig experience emotions such as being mad-
dened, perturbed, exasperated, and infuriated when
they encounter experiences that children sometimes
encounter. As young children listen to stories such
as these for a second or a third time, they can all
stand up and express the actions or emotions of the
story nonverbally.

Follow up the reading and pantomiming sessions with talk sessions in which the youngsters tell about when they were mad or what they did during the last snow storm. Young children can tell about their "mad day" or their "snow fun" pictorially by drawing their experiences.

At an upper level, groups of children who have had considerable experience with pantomiming and who have all read the same story, can select a short episode from the story to perform nonverbally as a book-sharing activity. The doughnut episode in Robert McCloskey's *Homer Price* (Viking, 1943, 1972), the tea party-on-the-ceiling episode in *Mary Poppins* (Harcourt Brace, 1972), the escape scene in *Mrs. Frisby and the Rats of NIMH* (Atheneum, 1971), or most any episode from *Henry and Beezus* (Morrow, 1952) or *Pippi Longstocking* (Viking, 1950, 1969) provide excellent material for short pantomimes in which children who have read a book try to interest others in it. At the same time, children who are refining their emerging pantomiming skills have a chance to try more demanding pantomime.

COMEDY SKITS   Brief descriptions of comic situations can be printed on slips of paper and placed in a grab bag. A volunteer draws a slip of paper from the bag and pantomimes the situation using exaggerated motions that will make the action funny. Possible descriptions include:

- Someone suffering from an aching tooth.
- Someone trying to drive off and catch a bothersome fly or mosquito.
- Someone trying to walk on slippery ice who keeps losing his balance.

* A woman wearing a mini-skirt trying to pick up a piece of paper.
* Someone trying not to sneeze.
* Someone trying to open a locked door when both arms are loaded with packages.

TEAM COMEDIES Humorous situations in which several youngsters participate nonverbally are advisable for children who feel more comfortable being part of a pantomiming group than being a sole comedian. Again descriptions of funny situations can be written on slips of paper and drawn from a hat by a team captain. Groups can work out their nonverbal skits before presenting them before the class; if they wish, they can even locate props to support their pantomime. Suggested situations are:

* A boy with an aching tooth goes to the dentist.
* A leak in a roof turns from a drip to a flood—you are all there!
* Three awkward boys try to carry a large pane of glass through a narrow hall, down a flight of stairs, and through a crowded room.
* A short person tries to see over the ever-moving head of an immense lady sitting in front of her.
* Three girls in the middle-section of a movie get up to buy popcorn, and after returning to their seats, cause chaos by eating it.

SYNCHRONIZE THE SOUND A sophisticated, fun form of pantomime requires synchronization between two children. One of the pair pantomimes a series of events, while his partner creates the sound effects associated with the actions. For example, the pantomimist conveys the impression that he is pouring water into a glass. He picks up an empty glass, holds it in the air, and wipes a fleck of dust out of it. Then he picks up a bottle of liquid, shakes it, and pours the liquid from the bottle to the glass. At the moment when the pantomimist begins to pour, his off-stage sound-effects confederate makes glug-glug-glug-glug pouring sounds, stopping at the precise instant that the pantomimist "turns" the bottle upright.

Other actions for synchronized sound-effects pantomiming are:

* Sneaking across a creaking floor.
* Walking in the dark, banging into objects, and stepping on the tail of a cat.
* Concocting something in the kitchen with all the noises and actions of cooking—the mixer, the refrigerator door, the running water.
* Knocking on and then opening a creaky door.
* Polishing a glass and then dropping it with a resounding crash and picking up the pieces.
* Constructing a piece of furniture with a hammer and saw.
* Learning to play a musical instrument—piano, violin, or saxophone.
* Chopping down a tree.
* Carrying a load of books, dropping one with a crash, picking it up with creaking legs, and then dropping another pile.

In each of these sequences, it is the sound-effects person who supplies the appropriate sounds that give reality to the pantomimist's actions and facial expressions.

Youngsters who have a fine sense of humor enjoy

this activity, for the most effective pantomimes are those spiced with a pinch of humor—humor conveyed by exaggerated facial expressions, physical responses, and sound effects. It is the kind of pantomiming at which Flip Wilson excels, and youngsters who have a knack for it may find that watching Flip supplies ideas for additional pantomiming sequences in which several students can interact.

PROVERBS　　Interpreting proverbs can provide a context in which children who have had some preliminary work with pantomiming can explore the communicative possibilities of body language. First, discuss the meaning of a proverb such as *A stitch in time saves nine* with the students. Help them to see both the literal and the figurative meaning of the proverb. Then encourage a number of children to interpret physically specific words in the proverb. Talk about and try out how *a stitch, time, saves,* and *nine* can be expressed nonverbally. Help children develop awareness of the intricacies of the message they are sending by carrying out actions on a large scale, e.g., making a big stitch and pulling through a large needle with a long thread. Help children to develop precision in their nonverbal expression of meanings by carrying out actions in slow motion, e.g. sticking in the needle and pulling it out in a way that shows the fabric is stiff.

Work as a total class on additional proverbs such as *Too many cooks spoil the broth*. Help children to analyze the actions implied in the words of the proverb; for example, ask, "What could each cook be doing?" As children propose possibilities suggest, "Let's try out that action!" The teacher can further encourage children to think about nonverbal expression by asking, "How could we show that the broth was spoiled?" and respond to suggestions with, "Let's try out that action."

After a period of discussion and trying out, divide the class into groups of three or four "cooks." Each group must work together to perfect a sequence of actions to dramatize the proverb. Again the teacher can stress "move slowly" and "make every action count" to develop precision in nonverbal expression. When each group has put together and tried out a sequence of motions, it can present its sequence for the entire class to enjoy.

On other occasions, study pantomiming sequences first as a total class activity, then as a small group activity, and finally as a presentation activity by groups to the class. Proverbs that serve this purpose well include:

> A penny saved is a penny earned.
> Don't count your chickens before they hatch.
> Don't put all your eggs in one basket.
> Don't cry over spilled milk.
> Plodding wins the race.

In each case talk about different ways to interpret physically the proverb and try out a number of different interpretations.

MIMICKING THE PROFESSIONAL   Children who take easily to pantomiming and find it to be their forte may enjoy imitating successful professional pantomimists. Jack Guilford, Flip Wilson, Red Skelton, and Laurel and Hardy all supply good, firsthand material that children can adapt. A standing assignment in an upper-elementary grade classroom can be to watch a professional at work on TV, to observe the details of his act, and then to try out the routine oneself. After several practice sessions, the youngster can perform his imitations before a classroom group.

BUILDING PANTOMIME BLOCKS In open-type classrooms in which children individually and co-operatively pursue learnings related to their unique interests and needs, one option that can always be open to an individual or to a group of youngsters is building pantomime blocks—creative sequences of motions that tell a story or depict some action. In more highly structured classrooms, the teacher can add this activity as an option to be chosen during independent study or seatwork periods.

To build a pantomime block, an individual simply thinks through an incident—make-believe or real—and devises a sequence of motions to communicate the happening to others. A group working together talks about an incident, brainstorming the kinds of movements necessary to tell others their story nonverbally. Then the individual or group privately tries out his or their original pantomime.

A listing of motions, characters, places, and times can help to start children inventing the stories based on pantomime blocks. Such a listing can be presented on a bulletin board display captioned: Building Blocks for Pantomime.

TUESDAY

7

MARCH						
S	M	T	W	T	F	S
1	2	3	4	5	6	7
8	9	10	11	12	13	14
15	16	17	18	19	20	21
22	23	24	25	26	27	28
29	30	31				

MAY						
S	M	T	W	T	F	S
					1	2
3	4	5	6	7	8	9
10	11	12	13	14	15	16
17	18	19	20	21	22	23
24	25	26	27	28	29	30
31						

APR. 1981

8:00

8:30

9:00

9:30

10:00

10:30

11:00

11:30

12:00

1:00

1:30

2:00

2:30

3:00

3:30

4:00

4:30

5:00

5:30

MONDAY

APRIL						
S	M	T	W	T	F	S
			1	2	3	4
5	6	7	8	9	10	11
12	13	14	15	16	17	18
19	20	21	22	23	24	25
26	27	28	29	30		

6

APR. 1981

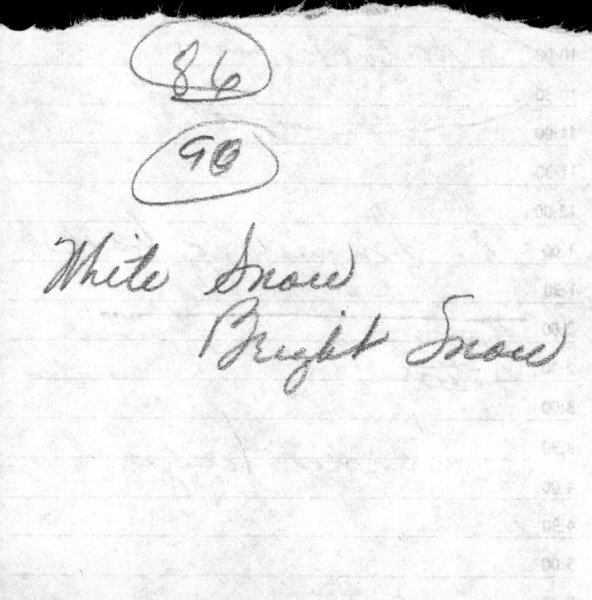

86

98

White Snow
Bright Snow

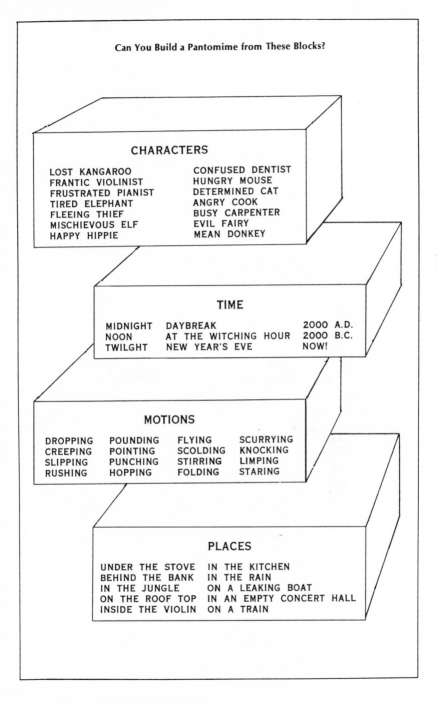

BULLETIN BOARD DISPLAY FOR BUILDING BLOCKS FOR PANTOMIME

Youngsters may select just one building block, e.g., a frustrated pianist, upon which to concoct a pantomime. Or they can select several blocks as a story base, e.g., a frustrated pianist, a frantic violinist, a mischievous elf, in an empty concert hall, at midnight. Or they can draw upon one building block idea such as on a leaking boat and think of additional ideas such as "the hopeful fish and the more hopeful fisherman."

After preparing a sequence, the pantomimist or pantomimists can present the act before a group or the entire class. The pantomimist can use a musical accompaniment supplied by records or even by a fellow student who can play an instrument. If the story to be told becomes complex, a narrator can be added to fill in transitional details.

PANTOMIMING MESSAGES

SMILE FOR THE CAMERA   This activity is useful in focusing students' attention on the meaning of facial expressions. The teacher asks such questions as:

What is a grin?	What is a wink?
What is a sneer?	What is a grimace?
What is a scowl?	What is a frown?
What is a smile?	What is a smirk?

Children respond not with words but by facial expressions. Children can then use words to talk about what message each expression conveys.

If the school owns a camera, this is a fine time to expose a roll of film. Line up all the children. Everybody grin! Snap a picture. Do the same with every one frowning, then with everyone winking, then with everyone sneering. If you have enough film, take pictures of all the children showing they don't like something, showing they do like something, or showing boredom.

Mount the photographs on the bulletin board with captions made by pupil teams that read, "Here we are when we feel _____."

CREATE AN IMPRESSION Print situations on individual cards, such as:

You want someone to think you are not afraid.
You want someone to think you are enjoying yourself.
You want someone to think you are very busy.
You want someone to think you are in a hurry.
You want someone to think you know what you are
doing.

Distribute the impression cards to individuals who volunteer to try to create the impression described on the card. Other children must decide what kind of an impression each pantomimist is trying to communicate.

To simplify the activity, write all the impression situations on the board. Guessers can match a written impression with a pantomimist's activity. To involve more children, distribute several cards with the same situation. Each tries his hand at creating the impression.

WHAT AM I SAYING Write sets of related sentences on the board; a child selects one to pantomime as others watch and guess. Use such sentences as:

- He was very attentive.
  He paid no attention.
  He paid only a little attention.

- He enjoyed what was going on.
  He hated every moment of it.
  He was only half-hearted
  about what was going on.

- The little girl was afraid of the dog.
  The little girl loved the dog.
  The little girl ignored the dog.

- I am disgusted.
  I am proud.
  I am angry.

If a child thinks he knows which sentence a pantomimist has acted out, he raises his hand. The pantomimist must indicate which student he wants to answer through some nonverbal action; the student chosen comes forward and points to the sentence he thinks is the one being expressed. The pantomimist must indicate correct or incorrect nonverbally. If the student has selected the correct sentence, he becomes the pantomimist; if not, another student is indicated nonverbally, and he selects.

Note: The entire game is played wordlessly; gestures and facial expressions indicate whether a guess is correct, who is to participate, and when.

BODY TALK Print pantomime cards in sets of three such as the following:

- Believe you are washing windows.
  Let your body say you are really trying to do a good job.

Let your body say you hate the job.

Let your body say that you are rushing the job to get to something else.

* Believe you are standing in line.

Let your body say you are waiting to have a flu shot.

Let your body say you are waiting to go to an exciting movie and you can hardly wait.

Let your body say you are tired waiting.

* Believe you are chopping wood.

Let your body say that you are very tired, but you are determined to get the job done anyway.

Let your body say that you have lots of energy and are eager to do the job. You enjoy it.

Let your body say that you are being required to do the task and you don't like it.

* Believe you are listening to a person speak to you.

Let your body say that you disagree violently with the speaker.

Let your body say you are really in agreement with the speaker.

Let your body say you are having trouble staying awake.

Display simultaneously the three cards of a set. A child mentally selects one card and "let's his body talk." Other children guess which feeling the pantomimist is trying to express. Again, conduct the guessing activity nonverbally.

This activity can be a prelude to a talk-time in which children relate incidents from their own lives in which they sensed when someone liked something by the person's nonverbal reactions.

After children have played at body talk, encourage small groups of children to devise other "Believe you are . . . Let your body say . . ." episodes that can be expressed nonverbally in future games. Pupil teams can print up the pantomime cards before the activity. In doing this, youngsters are forced to think about situations in which the body talks.

YES, NO, AND MAYBE! It is very possible to say yes, no, and maybe nonverbally using gestures, facial expressions, and/or full body motion. To help children express these meanings physically, divide them into pupil teams (about five to a team). Each child in a team draws a yes, no, or maybe slip from a hat. These slips carry instructions such as: "Say *no* as if you really meant it." "Say *no* as if you could be persuaded to change your mind." "Say *yes* as if you really meant it." "Say *yes* as if you feel you must, but you would really prefer not to." "Say *maybe*." There should be enough slips in the hat for every child. (There will be duplicates, of course.)

In groups, each child expresses the reaction he has selected without relying on words; others in the group analyze his performance and guess what it is he is trying to say without words.

HELLO THERE! To investigate the nonverbal ways that people "say" hello, good-bye, and how do you do, the class divides into two action groups. Each group lines up and faces the other across a distance of about three feet. Then the teacher can call out interaction directions:

• Pretend you see a friend at a distance. Say hello without using words.

- Pretend you are meeting the person opposite you, walk toward him, and say how do you do without using words.
- Pretend you are saying good-bye to the person opposite you; do so wordlessly.

As each direction is given, a youngster communicates that meaning to the person opposite him. Try each encounter several times so that the children can try other techniques; you may find it wise to move the line at each try so that each child works with several partners.

After children have tried out the three social encounters with different partners, involve them in a discussion of the ways people tend to say hello, good-bye, and how do you do. Make a chart like the one shown below:

HELLO	GOOD-BYE	HOW DO YOU DO

As children identify gestures or facial expressions people use to communicate these meanings, list them on the chart, which can later be mounted on the bulletin board.

Send children on a magazine picture hunt to search for pictures showing people greeting one another nonverbally. These pictures can be mounted on the bulletin board with lines connecting each picture to the appropriate caption on the chart. Encourage children to search for pictures depicting people of different cultures greeting one another, e.g., formal bowing. Through this activity children may become more aware that a gesture system has its origins in the society in which it is used and that gestures do not carry precisely the same meaning to all people.

SUMMARY THOUGHTS

The activities described in this chapter are merely suggestive of the numerous kinds of experiences that can be designed into the elementary school program. None needs to be carried out precisely as described. You—the teacher—may want to modify an activity to meet the unique requirements of your classroom situation. You may want to redesign an activity to make it more sophisticated for use with older students or to modify a sequence to make it less sophisticated for use with little children.

Then too, ideas for expressing meanings through pantomime can be introduced by the teacher in the context of many classroom experiences. Children involved in a spelling or vocabulary development activity can *show* meanings of words with which they are working rather than simply relying on verbal definitions. As part of a reading lesson youngsters can *show* the story action to convey their understanding rather than answering all comprehension questions verbally. Children telling about a TV program they enjoyed can *show* part of the action, and youngsters can share with their friends some episodes from individually read books using the language of their bodies.

As implied in the opening section of this chapter, the purpose of encouraging nonverbal expression is not to turn each child into a professional pantomimist. Instead the ultimate goal is to develop children's awareness of the communicative potential of body language, to free inhibitions about physical expression of meanings, and to build children's skill in communicating with more than words.

III: TURN ON the SOUND

For a child who often transports himself into the world of let's pretend, dramatic activity is an enjoyable form of self-expression. Yet from an educational perspective, dramatic activity offers more than fun. Through dramatization a child or youth encounters both the verbal and nonverbal components of communication. Acting out requires a child to vary the pitch, loudness, or tone of voice as he becomes someone else. Acting out compels him to produce body motions he typically does not use. It may force him into greater awareness of his potential to express meanings vocally and physically and into an awareness of the kinds of messages he himself receives through actions and words.

In this chapter several kinds of dramatic activity through which youngsters can encounter verbal/ nonverbal expression are presented. First is a series of activities termed pre-dramatic play—structured experiences designed to increase skill in using the body and voice to heighten a verbal communication. In pre-dramatic play children experiment with vocal and action-filled interpretations without the pressure of preparing words and actions for a full-blown audience-type performance. Second is a series of ideas for "Show Times"—low key, classroom productions given for the enjoyment of classmates. While preparing "Show Times," youngsters apply the skills being developed in more structured activities. Third, are role-playing experiences in which children work within everyday, social situations and improvise words and actions to develop a heightened understanding of communication.

These activities are *not* designed to turn children

into junior actors or to produce letter-perfect staged productions. When children become pawns, manipulated by teachers to produce mini-Broadway shows, very often the educational potential of dramatization goes unrealized. As set forth in this chapter, dramatization is simply the vehicle or means through which children build communication skills.

PRE-DRAMATIC PLAY

PLAY-TIME For the very young child, pre-dramatic play can be the unstructured, self-initiated activities of creative play. Set up a let's pretend corner in the kindergarten and first grade where two or three children can play together at pretending. Make available in the corner things to encourage creative play activity:

- Hard rubber animals—alligators, owls, giraffes, turtles, snakes.
- Play trucks, cars, service stations.
- Doll houses, furnishings, and several miniature dolls to be moved through the house.
- Snoopy, Big Bird, Mean Oscar, and Pogo dolls.

Encourage young children to talk about these let's pretend items while they are holding the objects; usually a child will not only tell about the toy but actually show how the truck, alligator, or dolls move about.

PRE-DRAMATIC PLAY WITH STORIES Before children are ready to participate in longer, self-directed dramatizations, they need numerous opportunities to play with the verbal, vocal, and physical elements of dramatization in a semi-structured

situation. The teacher who expects groups of youngsters to design and execute a dramatization before
they have had preliminary opportunities to play with
the specific elements of dramatic expression may
find that the children really do not know where to
begin and end up simply being silly.

Pre-dramatic play can begin with a teacher-cen-
tered, storytelling experience. Tell a story such as
the *Three Billy Goats Gruff* (see Marcia Brown's picture book published by Harcourt, Brace, if you don't
remember the tale). After telling the story in an
expressive way, chalk out on the floor the bridge
that the three billy goats have to cross to reach the
field of lush grass. Tell the children to *believe* that
the chalked area is the bridge. Have two big signs
ready, one marked "Bare Mountain," the other
"Grassy Meadow." Student volunteers hold up the
signs, one on each side of the bridge, to define these
areas as the important locales in the story.

Now initiate the pre-dramatic play. Ask for a child
volunteer to show how Little Billy Goat Gruff must
have walked across the bridge; let several youngsters give their interpretations. Other children can
show how the middle-sized goat must have walked
across the bridge; others demonstrate how Big Billy
Goat Gruff must have strutted across. The children
demonstrate by actually coming up to the marked-
off bridge and walking across it. Encourage children
to talk about how the players physically expressed
the differences between the three goats. All the children can form a line of little billy goats and cross
the bridge in turn; they can do the same with the
middle- and large-sized goats.

Next all the children can crouch down by their

desks and pretend to be the troll who lives under
the bridge; they jump up just as the troll must have
jumped up. Ask the children if they recall the words
the troll spoke as he jumped out in front of Little
Billy Goat Gruff. Decide what words he spoke and
talk about how he must have uttered them. Did he
shout them? whisper them? say them slowly or
quickly? Did he say them cruelly? with scorn? with
friendliness?

Put an X on the bridge; when the little goat reaches
that spot, all the other children hop up from under-
neath their desks and call out the words of the troll.
Try this several times to give the children the feeling
that they are really trolls.

See if the children can recall the words spoken by
the little billy goat; let them try out those lines.
Volunteers can speak the lines using soft, medium,
scared, or self-assured voices. They accompany their
words with facial expressions that show how the
goat must have felt. Continue this way through the
five or six major events of the fairy tale with volunteers speaking the words of the goats and the troll.

Then ask for volunteers for a first run-through of
the entire story. In this first run-through, you—the
teacher—serve as narrator, telling the beginning of
the story and adding the ending. Children take the
parts of the troll and the three billy goats.

On another day, return to the same story. Start the
pre-dramatic play by asking children to show again
the way the goats walked, the way the troll jumped
up, the way the goats spoke, and the way the troll
spoke. Select several volunteers for a second run-
through; ask whether there is a child who remem-

bers the story well enough that he or she can be the narrator. Run through the story several times so that many children can participate. Use the same simple props—a chalked bridge and signs indidcating the bare mountain and the grassy meadow.

Do the same kind of pre-dramatic work, which emphasizes using the body and voice expressively, with other action stories that children like. With young children stories such as "Jack and the Beanstalk," "The Emperor's New Clothes," "The Three Bears," and "The Three Little Pigs" can be the basis for pre-dramatic play. With older children, more sophisticated stories, such as myths, are good for pre-dramatic interpretation, and several excellent anthologies are available. Charles Kingsley's *The Heroes* (Dutton, 1963) is a fine source as are Padraic Column's two books, *The Golden Fleece and the Heroes Who Lived Before Achilles* (Macmillan, 1962) and *The Children's Homer: Adventures of Odysseus and the Tale of Troy* (Macmillan, 1962), and Ingri and Edgar Parin d'Aulaire's *D'Aulaires' Book of Greek Myths* (Doubleday, 1962). You can encourage children to read some of the myths in these volumes so that they know the plot, or you can tell a myth or read it to them. The telling or reading is a springboard to dramatic interpretation in the manner described above.

You can also make available books that contain a single myth. For instance, there is Penelope Proddow's recent retelling of the story of the abduction of Persephone, daughter of Demeter, the goddess who controls the seasons: *Demeter and Persephone* (Doubleday, 1972, illustrated by Barbara Cooney).

There is Nathaniel Hawthorne's version of the tale of the king with the power to turn everything he touches to gold: *The Golden Touch* (McGraw-Hill, 1959, illustrated by Paul Galdone). There are Ian Serraillier's versions of the tales of Heracles, Theseus, Jason, Perseus, and Daedalus (all Walck) in *Heracles the Strong* (1970, illustrated by Rocco Negri), *The Way of Danger: The Story of Theseus* (1963, illustrated by William Stobbs), *The Clashing Rocks: The Story of Jason* (1964, illustrated by William Stobbs), *The Gorgon's Head: The Story of Perseus* (1962, illustrated by William Stobbs), and *A Fall from the Sky: The Story of Daedalus* (1966, illustrated by William Stobbs). Serraillier tells these old-time favorites of Greek mythology in a marvelously poetic way. Each of his books can stimulate pre-dramatic play through which children gain skill in expressing meanings both physically and vocally.

Similar skills can be developed from dramatic interpretations of episodes from books read and reread by children and youth. An episode from Robert McCloskey's *Homer Price* (Viking, 1943, 1972), Astrid Lindgren's *Pippi Longstocking* (Viking, 1950, 1969), or even Robert Louis Stevenson's *Treasure Island* or *Kidnapped* can supply material to be expressed dramatically. With such material, as with the Billy Goat Gruff type of story, the format for the activity is:

- Expressive reading of the story silently by students or orally by the teacher or a student who has practiced reading the story (see Chapter 4).
- Trying out the major actions of the story. Individual

children volunteer and/or all the youngsters participating in the activity become the characters and play the parts.
- Trying out lines. Again, all the children play with the words of the story, interpreting them expressively.
- Assembling simple props.
- Preliminary run-through of the story with volunteers taking specific parts.
- Run-through of the nonverbal and verbal expression of the story on several later occasions.

Don't forget that running through pre-dramatic play can be an option that several children can select during independent work or study sessions. Groups of children who finish their quiet work can move into the hall to practice an episode from *Homer Price,* the story of Jason, or the tale of the emperor that they enacted as a class an earlier day.

PRE-DRAMATIC PLAY WITH PAPER BAG HAND PUPPETS   Puppets are a great device for helping children loosen up their vocal inhibitions. As a pre-dramatic play activity, give each child a paper bag to turn into Snoopy, Lucy, or Charlie Brown with the aid of colored crayons. After each child has drawn a figure on his bag, read and show to the class several *Peanuts* comic strips featuring these characters. Ask the children who have made a Snoopy puppet how they think Snoopy sounds when he speaks. Does he talk loudly? softly? sharply? gently? Does he have a high voice? a low voice? Does he sound bored? happy? content? disgusted? carefree? When children answer, ask them to demonstrate by saying some of Snoopy's comic strip lines while moving their paper bag puppets to simulate Snoopy's movements. Remind the children that when people talk, they often lean forward, turn their heads, and lift their chins. Suggest that they move their puppets in "people-action" as they talk for Snoopy.

Then have children discuss what kind of person Lucy is. As that kind of person how would she talk? Would she talk gently? sharply? in a pleasant tone of voice? How would she hold and move her body? Ask the children who have made Lucy puppets to speak some of Lucy's comic strip lines, moving their hand puppets to show her action. A similar sequence can be carried out for Charlie Brown.

When children have tried Lucy, Snoopy, and Charlie Brown voices and actions, call for volunteers to come forward to "play a strip." The volunteers can enact one of the strips the teacher read earlier in the session.

Keep a supply of short, two- or three-character comic strips (*Henry, Nancy, Blondie,* or *Pogo,* for example), small paper bags, and an assortment of colored flow pens available in the classroom. One follow-up activity during independent study sessions is to have two- or three-person teams of children choose a strip, determine who will become each character, make paper bag puppets of the characters, try out voices and actions, and "play a strip."

The advantages of pre-dramatic play with paper bag puppets are twofold. First, little time and few supplies are required to make puppets with paper bags. The activity can be initiated and carried through before children's interest wanes. Second, a child sometimes feels less inhibited when expressing himself behind the facade of a puppet who is speaking and moving. In addition, the child's person is hidden behind a screen, a desk, or a puppet stage.

There are advantages, too, in using comic strip characters for pre-dramatic play. Often children know these characters intimately; they know how a character tends to speak and act. Thus, the task is not difficult for them. Second, children associate pleasure with their comic strip friends, and because of this, the dramatization is fun.

TALKING ANIMALS AND HEAD PUPPETS Combining dramatic interpretation of talking animal stories with paper bag head puppets can provide the young child with further encounters with the elements of nonverbal communication—especially vocal elements. Each youngster participating in the activity works with a large, paper grocery bag. He staples a large piece of light-colored construction paper to the front and back of the bag.

Then he listens as the teacher or an upper-grade youngster (see Chapter 4) reads an animal story in which beasts talk just as people do. For kindergarten a fine choice is Marjorie Flack's *Ask Mr. Bear* (Macmillan, 1932, 1958). In the story a boy turns to a series of animals for advice on what to give his mother for her birthday. Mr. Bear supplies the right answer—a great, big bear hug.

After hearing the story, each child selects the animal he will be. One way to be certain that all characters are chosen by about equal numbers is to divide the class into sections equal to the number of characters in the story. Within each group, children draw lots to determine which story character to make and to become.

Next, children make their head puppets. They cut holes in their bags for eyes, nose, and mouth. They can turn up the bottoms of their bags, if they are too large for them to balance on their shoulders. With colored felt pens, they ink in facial features— eyelashes, eyebrows, cheeks, ears. Colored paper strips or pieces of shaggy yarn or carpet can be stapled on for hair.

When the head puppets are finished, you can reread the story; this time each child focuses on the lines and action of *his* character. Rather than following up directly with each child playing his part, schedule some pre-dramatic study. How do you think the small boy sounded as he spoke to each animal? Children who have made the little boy puppet heads demonstrate, wearing their heads. Will the little boy speak in the same way to each animal? Again children answer by demonstrating. How do you think the boy walks? gestures? Will he change his way of walking as he nears home? Once again the children pantomime rather than speak answers. Do the same kind of questioning, demonstrating with each of the story's characters; children give answers while wearing their puppet heads to get them into the story mood. This structured study is designed to give the children an opportunity to learn their lines as well as to help them develop skill in manipulating their voices and bodies.

Of course, schedule time for each group to run

through the entire story sequence. You may use simple signs such as "Home," "Bear's House" to define story locales. These run-throughs can occur on the same or preferably on successive days. Since young children enjoy hearing a story told and re-told, you will find that they generally listen as intently to the first group's rendition as to the last. Also, you will find that often each successive group's presentation improves in quality as children watch the motions of their friends, listen for vocal effects, and incorporate the most appropriate ones in their own performances. In this activity as in others designed as pre-dramatic play, do *not* emphasize the quality of the presentation. Rather, emphasize children's development of some control over their voices and bodies so that both become effective communication agents.

Other talking animal stories that can be utilized for similar pre-dramatic play experience include: Don Freeman's *Inspector Peckit* (Viking, 1972), Arnold Lobel's *Frog and Toad Are Friends* (Harper & Row, 1970), Else Minarik's *Little Bear* (Harper & Row, 1957) as well as other books in Ms. Minarik's "Little Bear" series, Hans A. Rey's *Curious George* (Houghton Mifflin, 1941) as well as other books in the series, Marcia Brown's *How, Hippo!* (Scribners, 1969), George Selden's *The Cricket in Times Square* (Farrar, Straus, 1960), and William Steig's *Sylvester and the Magic Pebble* (Simon and Schuster, 1969).

Talking animal stories appropriate for pre-dramatic play experiences for youngsters in the middle-elementary grades include picture books that add an ounce of humor such as Bernard Waber's *Lyle, Lyle, Crocodile* (Houghton Mifflin, 1965) and *Lovable Lyle* (Houghton Mifflin, 1969), and Scott Corbett's *Ever Ride a Dinosaur?* (Holt, 1969) as well as longer stories such as Richard Atwater's *Mr. Popper's Penguins* (Little, Brown, 1938), E. B. White's *Charlotte's Web* (Harper & Row, 1952), and Robert Lawson's *Rabbit Hill* (Viking, 1944). The more recent *Mrs. Frisby and the Rats of NIMH* by Robert O'Brien (Atheneum, 1971) combines both talking animals and science fiction in a tale, portions of which can be adapted for pre-dramatic experiences using paper bag head puppets. Working from books such as these, older children can concentrate on a single scene rather than attempting to dramatize the entire story.

NOISE WORDS Some sounds cry out to be "spoken" physically as well as vocally. Such a sound is "shhhhhhh." Children can:

- First, speak the sound without moving a single muscle.
- Second, speak the sound while leaning slowly toward the listener.
- Third, speak the sound while adding appropriate gestures, motions, or facial expressions.
- Fourth, speak the sound with accompanying gestures, motions, and expressions, but lower the voice until it is almost imperceptible.
- Fifth, speak the sound with different gestures and facial expressions, but raise the voice.
- Sixth, experiment with reproducing the sound in other ways.

Try similar expressive sequences with such sounds as:

Bbrrrrrrrrrrrrr	Eeeeeeehhhhhhhhh
Ooooooooohhhhhhhhh	Whoooooooops
Ooooowwwww	Yiiiikes
Wheeeeeeeeeee	Claaannnggg

By the way, this activity fits well in a reading experience. When children encounter sound words in the stories they are reading in small group reading sessions, they can experiment with different ways of uttering the sounds.

WORD STIMULI   Reacting verbally and nonverbally to specific word stimuli written into and repeated in a story is another form of pre-dramatic play. When children hear the stimulus word, they react with a physical and a verbal expression as rapidly as they can; the expression is one that they have determined in advance and repeat each time the stimulus word pops up in the story.

For example, teacher Lillian Lemke designed the following story with her students:

The Frontier Thanksgiving

Early one *Thanksgiving* morning. . . many years ago, on the old *Frontier*. . . a *Settler*. . . stood before his lonely *Cabin*. . . with his trusty *Gun*. . . and faithful *Dog*. . . ready to hunt the *Turkey*. . . he needed for *Thanksgiving* dinner, and hoping that no *Indians*. . . would spoil his feast. Whistling to his *Dog*. . . the *Settler*. . . shouldered his *Gun*. . . and started down the forest trail. Meantime, an *Indian*. . . with his *Gun*. . . and a *Dog*. . . approached down the forest trail from the other direction. Just at that moment a fat *Turkey*. . . flew between them. Off went the *Guns*. . . down fell the *Turkey*. . . in bounded the *Dogs*. . . up rushed the *Indian*. . . and the *Settler*. "It's mine," said the *Settler*. "Ugh-him mine," said the *Indian*.

"Grrrr," snarled the *Dogs*. And the noise of the argument shook the *Cabin*. . . and woke the whole *Frontier*. But the *Turkey*. . . who was only stunned by the blast of the *Guns*. . . , took off unsteadily and flew in the open door of the *Cabin*. . . where it was promptly captured by the *Indian*. . . and the *Settler*. . . and the *Dogs*. And thus, Thanksgiving was shared in a lonely *Cabin*. . . on the *Frontier*.[1]

Whenever a word listed in the left-hand column on the chart below appeared in the story, Ms. Lemke's students reacted with the words and actions noted in the other columns. The students themselves invented the verbal and nonverbal responses indicated.

Verbal and Nonverbal Responses to The Frontier Thanksgiving

Character	Verbal Response	Nonverbal Response
Settler	"Davy Crockett"	Stand and salute
Gun	"Bang! Bang!"	Stand up and sit down
Dog	"Man's best friend"	Wag arm
Turkey	"Yum, yum"	Flap arms
Cabin	"Shut the door"	Slam door in pantomime
The Frontier	"Way out West"	Spread arms
Indian	"Geronimo"	Pull bow
Thanksgiving	"Turkey day"	Pat tummy

Of course, the final rendition of a word-stimulus story may appear "put-on" or "canned;" after all,

---

[1] Quoted by permission of Lillian Lemke.

the motions and words are completely predetermined, and everyone reacts in the same way. There is a purpose, however, with such word-stimuli stories. Children have fun reacting quickly; they loosen their inhibitions in this unison, game-like setting; and they begin to relate meanings to be expressed with nonverbal activity. Some children may find it easy to write other stories that can be responded to verbally and nonverbally in the same way. Individually or cooperatively these youngsters can prepare a story complete with verbal and nonverbal responses for later class use.

CHORAL SPEAKING—LET'S GET OUR BODIES INTO THE ACT Typical choral-speaking activities involve group oral interpretation of a written piece, but putting the body into the act can add another dimension to the interpretive process and help children find enjoyment in body movement. Take, for instance, the choral-speaking interpretation of "Hickory, Dickory, Dock" that teachers have been using for years and that is described by James Smith in *Adventures in Communication: Language Arts Methods* (Allyn and Bacon, 1972), and by Ethel Bridge in an article entitled "Hickory Dickory Dock: Prelude to Choral Speaking" in the December 1972 issue of *Elementary English*. After children have listened to the verse, they speak the lines in unison as if they were a big, loud grandfather clock. When children have run through the selection several times, the teacher asks, "What does the grandfather clock say?" The typical student answer is, "Tick, tock, tick, tock!" Now the class tries chorusing "Tick, tock, tick, tock, tick, tock . . ." as loudly and as strongly as the stately old grandfather clock. Then a group of children becomes the grandfather clock and choruses, "Tick, tock, tick, tock . . ." as the other youngsters chant the nursery rhyme. To increase oral interpretation during successive repetitions, the following variations can be attempted:

- The large group and small group vocally show that the clock is winding down.
- A second small group becomes a cuckoo clock and chants "Cuckoo! Cuckoo! Cuckoo!" as the first small group continues chanting "Tick, tock, tick, tock," and the large group says the rhyme.
- Another group becomes the gong and interjects "boong" after the chorus recites "The clock struck one."

Each of these variations relies on sound effects for its success. Now try physical effects! The children become the clock, putting their arms straight down in front of them with hands clasped to simulate the pendulum. As they chorus the verse, they swing their arms pendulum-style to the rhythm of lines that almost beg to be expressed physically. The children who become cuckoo clocks jut their arms in quick forward motions to simulate the motion of the cuckoo coming out of the clock. Or as the gong strikes one, children make a striking motion with their hands. Children themselves can invent a myriad of other physical and vocal interpretations to accompany the rhyme.

In the above mentioned article, Ms. Bridges recommends two other poems for creative expression: Laura Richards' "The Monkeys and the Crocodile" and "There Was Once a Puffin." Those, as well as "My Donkey" from Rose Fyleman's *Picture Rhymes from Foreign Lands* (Dover, 1971), work well with younger children. "My Donkey" is particularly fun to do, for children must perform the antics of the donkey who fakes his ailments. Of course, a Mother Goose collection supplies a host of choral-speaking selections that lend themselves to physical interpretations ranging from such old time favorites as "Ride a Cock Horse," "Tom, Tom, the Piper's Son," "Little Miss Muffet," and "Humpty Dumpty" to less well-known rhymes like "A Farmer Went Trotting":

A Farmer Went Trotting

A farmer went trotting upon his gray mare;
   Bumpety, bumpety, bump!
With his daughter behind him so rosy and fair;
   Lumpety, lumpety, lump!
A raven cried "Croak!" and they all tumbled down;
   Bumpety, bumpety, bump!
The mare broke her knees, and the farmer his crown;
   Lumpety, lumpety, lump!
The mischievous raven flew laughing away,
   Bumpety, bumpety, bump!
And vowed he would serve them the same the next day;
   Lumpety, lumpety, lump!

To this selection, youngsters can trot and tumble, bump and lump. By the way, how does one "lump"? Children can show you!

Two favorites that individual children can spontaneously interpret are Myra Cohn Livingston's "Wide Awake" and Karla Kuskin's "Spring." Both are chock-full of action words that almost demand physical interpretation:

Wide Awake

I have to jump up
   out of bed
   and stretch my hands
   and rub my head,
   and curl my toes
   and yawn
   and shake
   myself
   all wide awake!

Spring

I'm shouting
I'm singing
I'm swinging through the trees
I'm winging skyhigh
With the buzzing black bees.
I'm the sun
Im the moon
I'm the dew on the rose.
I'm a rabbit
Whose habit
Is twitching his nose.
I'm lively
I'm lovely
I'm kicking my heels.
I'm crying "Come dance"
To the fresh water eels.
I'm racing through meadows
Without any coat
I'm a gamboling lamb
I'm a light leaping goat.
I'm a bud
I'm a bloom
I'm a dove on the wing.
I'm running on rooftops
And welcoming spring!

And don't forget Vachel Lindsay's "The Potatoes' Dance" into which children can build an echo effect and his "The Mysterious Cat" to which children can creep cat-like. In Christina Rossetti's "Mix a Pancake" children can mix, stir, fry, toss, catch, and can just have fun!

So make this a fun activity. Encourage children to improvise. Let each child do his own thing spontaneously after some initial group experiences like "Hickory, Dickory, Dock." Fun is the name of the game!

BODY CHANTS   Children can extend their interest in choral speaking to a similar activity—body chants. In body chanting youngsters express the motions of play activity as they chant in unison activity poems that deal with motions of play. Here are several activity poems to use for body chants:

Bouncing

Bounce the ball
    and swing your leg;
Bounce the ball
    and swing your leg.

One time over
Two times over
Three times over
Four!

Whoops, you missed it!
Didn't catch it!

Try once more.

In "Bouncing" children pretend to bounce a ball and swing their legs over it as they chant the piece.

Hide and Seek

One, two, three, four,
Five, six, seven, eight,
Nine,
Ten,
Eleven,
Twelve!

Ready or not, here I come.
Looking here.
Looking there.
Not here.
Not there.

Stopped short.
Found you.
Down behind the garbage can.

Run for home!
You're out!

In "Hide and Seek" children can hide their heads as they count, they can move their heads from side to side to simulate a looking action, they can hunch down behind the garbage can, they can use facial expressions to show that they have found someone's hiding place, and they can run in place. The actions of their bodies clarify the words they are chanting.

Safe

"Play ball!" the umpire yelled,
and then, "Ball one!" "Ball two!"

I swung.
"Strike one!"

I swung.
"Strike two!"

I swung.
A hit!

Raced to first.
Dashed to second.
Lunged for third.

Was I out?
Was I safe?

Safe! A three-base hit!

In "Safe" youngsters mimic the fist-wielding antics of an umpire, the swinging of a batter, and the racing, dashing, and lunging of the runner. Here again their body movements clarify the words of the action piece they are chanting.

Jump Rope

Jump rope under.
Jump rope over.

Faster! Faster! Turn the rope.
Faster! Faster! Jump the rope.

Turn it fast.
Turn it slow.

Jump it high.
Jump it low.

You tripped— It tangled.
Start again.

In "Jump Rope" youngsters turn a rope and jump faster and faster until they trip. Their action, of course, is a pantomime "chanted" physically as they chant the piece orally.

Young children can also walk, step lightly, trot, skip, creep, run, and hop to the rhythm of other poems in which the action is less overt, but the rhythm sets the mood. After children have participated in body chants such as those described, the activity can stimulate them to write their own action poetry, which later they can turn into body chants. Among the action games they can write body chants for are jacks, hopscotch, potato-sack race, or catch. As a class or in small groups children can simultaneously chant and physically interpret the actions of their poems.

As with the choral-speaking activities previously suggested, body chanting is not a performance-type activity in which youngsters perform motions at predetermined spots in a poem. Overly practiced chants in which the motions are planted and performed on cue serve no function and very often appear unnatural to an audience. The emphasis in body chanting, in this writer's view, should be on creative expression, both physical and vocal.

JUMP ROPE CHANTS   The rhymes that youngsters chant as they jump rope can be a springboard to more expressive motions than are typically used when skipping rope.

For the teacher who wishes to explore the possibilities of adding more expressive motions to jump rope activities, Emma Worstell's *Jump the Rope Jingles* (Macmillan, 1967) is very useful. It is full of jingles that can be used not only for jumping rope but also can be converted into simple body chants.

An example of a jump rope chant is given by Kathleen Scholl in an article entitled "Children's Folklore—Experienced, Expressed, Retold" in the February 1973 issue of *Instructor* (p. 70):

> Room for rent.
> Inquire within.
> When I move out. . .
> You move in.
> Mabel, Mabel, set the table.
> Don't forget the salt and PEPPERS!

Ms. Scholl, a sixth-grade teacher in Bryan, Texas, reminds the reader that peppers "is a jump-rope word asking for the fastest turning of the rope possible." The child jumping must jump as fast as he can when he reaches that word. But at other points in the jingle—at the words "inquire," "move out," and "set the table"—the jumper can add hand gestures to his jumping activity. Since the jumper is already in a highly active state, adding more motion can make the game even faster, more difficult, and much more fun.

RIGMAROLE ACTION   A rigmarole is a counting chant that derives its appeal from the alliterative sounds of the rhyme and from the fact that before each new line is said, all preceding lines must be repeated. The best-known rigmarole is probably the Christmas song about "a partridge in a pear tree, two turtle doves, three French hens, four calling birds, five golden rings. . . ." Another is given by Charles Potter in *More Tongue Tanglers and a Rigmarole* (World Publishing, 1964):

One old ostrich
Two tree-toads twisting tendrils
Three tiny titmice tapping trees
Four fat friars fanning
Five fluffy finches flying fast
Six of Susie's sisters sewing shirts
Seven sea shells in Sarah's shawl
Eight elfs eating Easter eggs
Nine nimble noblemen nibbling nuts
Ten throbbing thrush thriving thither

Charles Potter suggests that the leader begin by reciting the first line. Each player tries to repeat it. Then the leader recites the next line, and players repeat both lines in sequence. With each successive line, the players repeat all preceding lines in the order given before saying the new line.

In verbal rigmaroles such as the ones given by Potter or "The Twelve Days of Christmas," children can add gestures as they say the lines. The Potter lines are filled with action words—tapping, twisting, fanning, flying, sewing, eating, nibbling, throbbing—that can be expressed nonverbally.

Rigmaroles are easy for children to compose and, because of the element of the ridiculous inherent in the jingles, fun as well. Start with a line such as "I saw one woman washing," which can be expressed simultaneously with nonverbal action. A youngster can repeat the beginning line and add an original second line: "I saw one woman washing, two terrifying tigers talking." A third child repeats the lines and adds a third, complete, of course, with nonverbal expression.

Once youngsters have experienced a rigmarole, writing a complete ten-line or twelve-line rigmarole can be an option that youngsters can select during independent study periods. Since the pleasure of a rigmarole comes from the sound of the piece as well as from its foolish meaning, the youngster may opt to compose his rigmarole on the tape recorder. He tries out lines by saying them into the recorder and then listening to his composition in play-back. Later he can assume the role of leader and share his action rigmarole with the class.

RIGMAROLE TAKE-AWAY A fun approach to rigmaroles is to take away a word already known to participants and substitute a gesture for that word. For instance, in the Potter rigmarole "One Old Ostrich," instead of speaking the word "old," youngsters say "old" nonverbally through gestures placed in the pause created by omitting the word. Once the youngsters get the hang of rigmarole take-away, they can substitute gestures for other words; they can hold up fingers to communicate the numbers rather than say "one," "two," "three. . ."

FINGER PLAYS Finger plays are part of children's folklore. Handed down from generation to generation, their origins are hidden in the past. Finger plays appeal to the young child because of his natural affinity for things that move and because of his feel for words that tickle tongue and ear. In a finger play, youngsters use their fingers and sometimes their bodies to interpret the action words of a rhyme they are speaking.

One old-time favorite is "The Eensy, Weensy Spider":

The eensy, weensy spider climbed up the water spout.
Down came the rain and washed the spider out.
Out came the sun and dried up all the rain.
So the eensy, weensy spider climbed up the spout again.

Children touch thumbs and opposite fingers to simulate climbing motion as they sing the first and last lines. Fingers make sprinkling motions on the second line, and on the third, upward motions of the arms express the sun coming out. After expressing the spider play with the traditional set of gestures, children can go on to invent their own original gestures.

A well-known favorite is "Where Is Thumbkin?" which is generally sung to the tune of "Frere Jacques":

Where is Thumbkin?
Where is Thumbkin?
Here I am!
Here I am!
How are you today, sir?
Very well, I thank you.
Run away.
Run away.

The second stanza begins "Where is Pointer?" The third starts with "Where is Middle Finger?" The fourth is about Ring Finger and the last is about Pinkie. The action sequence for the finger play consists of putting the hands behind the back on the first two lines, bringing out first one thumb and then the other on the lines "Here I am," bending down one thumb on the fifth line, bending down the other thumb on the next line, and making each thumb disappear behind the back on the last two lines.

This finger play can be made more expressive by drawing with red and blue ballpoint pens, eyes, nose, and mouth on each finger. A tiny finger hat can be constructed out of a piece of thin cardboard and stuck on each finger with scotch tape. Faces can also be drawn on the fingers of old white work gloves worn for the finger play.

Some finger plays involve larger expressive motions of the body. "The Little Teapot" is one of these:

> I'm a little teapot, short and stout.
> This is my handle.
> This is my spout.
> When I get excited, then I shout,
> *Tip me over! Pour me out!*

Young children make a handle by putting one hand on a hip, make a spout by extending the other arm "spout-like," and tip their bodies to pour out the tea.

There are many, many finger plays like these for the young child. Most teachers know "This is the church. This is the steeple. . . .", "Pat a cake, pat a cake. . .", and "Pease porridge hot, pease porridge cold. . ." For less familiar finger plays, Violette Steiner and Roberta Pond's *Finger Play Fun* (Charles Merrill, 1970) is a gold mine of clearly described finger plays for use with youngsters in first grade, kindergarten, and nursery school. Finger play pleasure is generally restricted to children in these lower grades.

FEELING THE SONG Children can not only get involved physically in poems but the action of music as well. Children can sing and

* March to "The Caissons" or "Marching Along Together."
* Jiggle the reins of Santa's reindeer to "Here Comes Santa Claus."
* Skip to "Pass Me By."
* Row to "Row, Row, Row Your Boat."
* Creep to "Tonight's the Night the Teddy Bears Have a Picnic."

Children can play at being "Song detectives" by listening to the TV and radio for songs that they can sing and simultaneously interpret physically.

SHOW TIMES

FABLE FESTIVAL Share with children in middle- and upper-elementary grades some of Aesop's fables. This can be done by having individual children select a fable from an anthology such as Louis Untermeyer's *Aesop's Fables* (Golden Press, 1964), Joseph Jacob's *The Fables of Aesop* (Macmillan, 1964), Albert Cullum's *Aesop in the Afternoon* (Citation Press, 1972) or James Reeves' *Fables from Aesop* (Walck, 1962). All these have dialogue that is perfect for dramatic expression. Children can prepare the fables they have selected for oral reading to their classmates, so that all the youngsters in the class gradually become familiar with a number of fables. Children can also encounter the fables of Aesop in a color film that is part of the "Banks Street Reading Incentive Series" distributed by McGraw-Hill. In it Victor Borge reads from the Untermeyer collection.

Some Monday when the children are well versed in fables, divide them into three- or four-person teams. These teams can cooperate during the week's activity-study periods to: (1) select a fable, (2) choose roles, (3) decide on and construct simple props, and (4) prepare a short dramatization of the fable they have chosen.

Check with the groups during the week to give help where needed and to find out which fables have been chosen. You might give the names of the selected fables to a student skilled in manuscript lettering. He can decide an appropriate order in which the fables can be presented and print a listing on a stencil headed Play Bill. It can be decorated with sketches of fable characters supplied by another student skilled in art.

Schedule a rehearsal time on Thursday when groups can get together and work out final details. This is not a time for memorizing lines. Rather the children work from their understanding of the over-all story development, and each time spontaneously express the words and actions.

On Friday afternoon, schedule Show Time. To set the stage for the activity, you may want to keep available a large spotlight that revolves and produces different colored lights in sequence. You may also want to keep available a large sign:

SHOW TIME

MATINEE THIS AFTERNOON
FABLE FESTIVAL

The words SHOW TIME and Matinee This After-noon can be written directly on the sign; the name of the show, FABLE FESTIVAL, can be printed on a separate strip of paper and taped to the sign. In this way the sign can be used over and over again.

Mount the sign upright just inside the classroom door with the flashing light shining on it as a wel-come to the afternoon session. If you darken the room, the effect will be more striking and more motivating. The child who has designed and pre-pared the Play Bill can stand at the door distribut-ing the programs, which have been duplicated.

In the classroom children gather in their groups around the sides of the room, leaving the central area free for the performances. As each group takes its turn, it moves into the central area, thus simpli-fying the transition from one group to the next. This is basically theatre-in-the-round.

After all groups have performed, involve the class in a discussion of such questions as:

- How could we have used our voices to add to the effect?
- How could we have used our bodies to add to the effect?
- Was there sufficient motion? too much motion?

  or

- Do you want to have a repeat performance for our-selves in which we try out different vocal and physical effects?

  or even

- Do you want to perform our fable festival for the other fourth or fifth grade?

If the children want to share the festival with another class, they can be invited into the classroom for a Show Time. Again arrange the classroom for ease of performing; groups of players sit together and move into the central area when their turn comes.

A DR. SEUSS EXTRAVAGANZA The books of Theodor Geisel—better known to his readers as Dr. Seuss—have been delighting youngsters and oldsters for more than thirty years. Since the Seuss books are filled with actions and feelings, dramatizations of Dr. Seuss favorites can heighten skill in projecting actions and feelings and also increase understanding of the qualities to look for when selecting books to read.

To initiate the activity, for a number of weeks make available several copies of some Seuss books that children read or reread independently. Particularly fine for this purpose are: *The 500 Hats of Bartholomew Cubbins* (Vanguard, 1938), *Horton Hatches the Egg* (Random, 1940), *Horton Hears a Who!* (Random, 1954), *The Cat in the Hat* (Random, 1957), *The Lorax* (Random, 1971), *The King's Stilts* (Random, 1939), and *The Cat in the Hat Comes Back!* (Random, 1958).

At the end of the preliminary reading weeks, children in teams select a Dr. Seuss story to act out. Suggest to team members that before making a selection they read parts of several stories aloud to one another and then decide by voting.

When each group has chosen a book, allow time during a week or two for groups to:

1. Discuss who will take what roles. A narrator may make transitions easier in some stories so that someone may choose to be the narrator.
2. Try out actions. Suggest that the teams first have a "silent" run-through in which they play with various gestures, facial expressions, and larger motions of the body.
3. Add a verbal storyline. Children can improvise their lines as they go along, using the chosen book merely as a guide.
4. Construct a backdrop for scenery. The backdrop can be a bulletin board on which a series of drawings from the story are displayed or a simple mural on which large cut-outs of the cat, the elephant, hats, the lorax, or the mazie bird are stapled.
5. Locate a few simple props, including a musical recording to serve as a mood-setter.

Group acivity can take place during independent study periods. When involved in preliminary run-throughs, groups can move into the hall so that they can project vocally and experiment with body motions without disturbing more quiet, contemplative classroom work.

When each group is ready, stage a classroom Dr. Seuss Extravaganza. Books to be dramatized can be suspended with cords, mobile-style, from the lighting fixtures. Desks and chairs can be pushed back leaving a large open space in the center of the room. The flashing spotlight used for the Fable Festival can be focused on the backdrop constructed for the occasion. Students can sit on the floor in the middle of the room to watch and listen as each group takes its place before the backdrop to perform its Dr. Seuss story.

MORE EXTRAVAGANZAS   Dr. Seuss is not the only children's writer whose books can be the focus of a classroom extravaganza. With younger children, the books of Ezra Jack Keats can be used in a similar but, of course, slightly more structured, teacher-guided manner. Good Keats' titles to use include: *Goggles* (Macmillan, 1969), *Peter's Chair* (Harper & Row, 1967), *Whistle for Willie* (Viking, 1964), *Letter to Amy* (Harper & Row, 1968), and *Apartment Three* (Macmillan, 1971).

With younger children who need more guidance, the dramatic groups can be the same as the reading groups already functioning in the class. At the beginning of a reading period, group members can have part of a Keats' story read to them by the teacher and talk about how that story could be dramatized. On the spot, youngsters can improvise lines and actions until they have dramatized most of the story. Then parts can be chosen, and the children can go off by themselves into a corner of the room to enjoy several run-throughs of the story as they redramatize it for themselves.

When several groups of children have enjoyed such a dramatic experience, schedule an extravaganza—a simple sharing time in which groups present their stories for their classmates. Again to make the experience more pleasurable, integrate an art experience in which children draw or paint pictures to complement their stories. Pictures can be mounted on a bulletin board that can be used as a backdrop for the performances. Again, the experience can be a musical one with a recording played softly in the background to establish the story mood.

SILHOUETTE PLAY   Children can also dramatize a story behind a thin curtain. Lights placed behind the sheet-like curtain make players' action visible in silhouette to observers sitting in the darkness on the other side. If players move deliberately with short jerky motions, they resemble animation to observers.

The tales of Hans Christian Andersen are easy to share in simulated animation through silhouette play. A fine introduction to his material and the dramatic technique is the ten-minute, black-and-white film distributed by Contemporary Films, *The Gallant Little Tailor.* This film is an animated silhouette production that tells the story of the little tailor who killed seven with one blow. After viewing the film, groups can choose their own Hans Christian Andersen favorite to work out in animated silhouette-style from behind a lighted curtain.

To help children choose, make available some of the picture books based on Andersen fairy stories:

The Emperor's New Clothes, illustrated by Virginia Lee Burton (Houghton Mifflin, 1949). The story of the emperor who would not admit that he could not see his new clothes.

The Nightingale, translated by Eva Le Gallienne and illustrated by Nancy Burkert (Harper & Row, 1965). The story of the little bird who brought joy and health to the Emperor of China.

Thumbelina, illustrated by Adrienne Adams (Scribners, 1961). The tale of tiny Thumbelina who came from the center of a tulip.

The Ugly Duckling, illustrated by Adrienne Adams (Scribners, 1965). The transformation of the ugly duckling into a beautiful, graceful swan.

The Wild Swans, illustrated by Marcia Brown (Scribners, 1963). The tale of Elisa who tries to find a way to free her brothers from the spell that changed them into swans.

And keep in readiness illustrated anthologies that contain the best of Hans Christian Andersen:

Seven Tales by Hans Christian Andersen, translated by Eva Le Gallienne, illustrated by Maurice Sendak (Harper & Row, 1959). Seven tales: "The Fir Tree," "The Princess and the Pea," "Happy Family," "The Ugly Duckling," "The Darning Needle," "It's Absolutely True!" and "The Steadfast Tin Soldier."

Andersen's Fairy Tales, illustrated by Janusz Grabinski (Meredith Press, 1963). Thirty favorites illustrated in a way children will appreciate.

Andersen's Fairy Tales, illustrated by L. B. Smith (Macmillan, 1963). A collection of fifty-three Andersen favorites.

Encourage several groups to become involved with different fairy tales so that one afternoon the class can enjoy a number of favorites by a master storyteller as interpreted dramatically by classmates.

Silhouette dramatizations can also be produced with stick puppets. Puppets are cut out of stiff cardboard and attached to sticks or rods. The front of the puppet stage is covered with a sheet-like curtain, a light is placed behind the stage so that it can only shine through the curtain, and the rest of the room is darkened. Performers move their puppets behind the lighted cloth as they speak expressively for the puppet characters. Again, Hans Christian Andersen stories are excellent for dramatizing in this way.

STORIES WITHIN STORIES   Some books for children are a sequence of stories, each of which can provide substance for dramatization. One perfect example is Bernard Waber's *Nobody Is Perfick* (Houghton Mifflin, 1971). Expression-filled faces accompany such Waber stories as "Say Something Nice" and "That Was Some Daydream," which have lots of action that can be shown nonverbally. Individuals or groups can select a story from the book and prepare it for dramatic presentation during an informal Show Time on Friday afternoon.

Then there are numbers of books that revolve around the actions of a strong central personality. Peggy Parrish's "Amelia Bedelia" series is a case in point. Amelia Bedelia, the housemaid who has trouble handling the figurative meaning of words, is the center of action in *Amelia Bedelia, Thank You, Amelia Bedelia, Amelia Bedelia and the Surprise Shower, Come Back, Amelia Bedelia,* and *Play Ball, Amelia Bedelia* (all Harper & Row). A group of children can work with each of the books and prepare it for dramatization during a class Show Time.

BOOK SALE   As children independently read books for enjoyment, they can record their names on index cards kept in a card file. A child who has read Scott O'Dell's *Sing Down the Moon* (Houghton Mifflin, 1970), for instance, records his or her name on the *Sing Down the Moon* card in the file. When four or five youngsters have signed the card, they automatically become a group to "sell" the book to others.

The group meets and decides how it can develop a sales pitch. Rather than writing a script for the sale, group members talk about possible actions and words to use, try some of them out experimentally, choose parts, and volunteer to carry out related tasks such as locating background music, constructing props, and locating needed gadgets. They then go into the hall to put together spontaneously their lines and precise motions. Groups can schedule several practice sessions during seat work periods.

When a group is ready to "sell" its book, members write their names and the book's title on a sales chart kept in the room, so that their presentation, can be scheduled into the weekly activities.

Keep a poster available that announces:

BOOK SALE TODAY

WE ARE SELLING:

A group scheduled to sell gets out the sign and staples onto it a paper giving the title and author of the book that will be up for sale. The group posts the sign outside the classroom door before the session when it will "sell."

After the group has presented its cooperative sales pitch in which members have extolled the good points of the book, one youngster can become the auctioneer and auction off the book to the highest bidder. Children bid with fake paper money they keep for the purpose. Show children how to bid nonverbally by holding up a number of fingers, nodding their heads, and waving their hands. By the way, an auction is a great way to involve children nonverbally and it can be used in other contexts besides a book sale.

ROLE PLAYING

ACTION-CONVERSATION SKITS Action-conversation skits are improvised sequences of actions and words worked out by youngsters who are reacting to short written descriptions of a situation. In improvising, youngsters may try to introduce a little humor into their skits.

To prepare for action-conversations, print short descriptions of situations on index cards. Situations that work well have elements of both the controversial and the fantastic, as do, for instance, the following descriptions built around a pollution theme. The imaginary action conversations are between:

- The lungs of a man who is smoking a cigarette and the man himself.
- Three fish and a turtle who live in a polluted river.
- A garbage can, a man who has just littered, and a metal soda can.
- Smoky the Bear and two boys who are building a campfire.
- Three pelicans watching an oil slick come toward them.
- Three birds sitting on a roof as they smell the foul gases from a nearby chimney."[2]

Three- or four-person teams select situation cards. They are given only a limited time (not more than ten minutes) to talk among themselves about possible actions and words they will try and then they

[2] From *Content and Craft: Written Expression in the Elementary School* by Dorothy Grant Hennings and Barbara M. Grant (Prentice-Hall, 1973).

role play the situation. Sometimes if each player wears a simple sign indicating what or who he is, e.g., Pelican, children are less inhibited and more expressive.

MORE ACTION-CONVERSATION SKITS   Another way to approach the same activity is to list on a sheet various characters who could interact. Self-organized teams, working together during activity periods, select from the list the characters they will be, decide on a setting for their skit, and by improvising put together a skit. Characters who are real or fantastic prove workable for middle-grade children:

policeman	organ grinder	medicine man
grocer	silly monkey	lady bug
flying mouse	man from outer	magic pumpkin
teacher	space	boy
hippie	scientist	girl
junkie	rat	angry father
violinist	owl	talking pineapple
talking cuckoo	ghost	kind fairy
clock	witch	

For children who need more guidance, supply a second list to be used in conjunction with the first; the second list suggests what the characters are doing:

fighting	scaring someone	searching for
fleeing	complaining	something
experimenting	sneaking	praising
plotting	crawling	hiding something
stealing	flying	
quivering with	traveling to	
fright	the moon	

This type of activity can be enjoyed simply as an experience in self-expression; the youngsters on a team role play for themselves with no thought of sharing their performance with classmates.

ACTION-CONVERSATION MONOLOGUES An individual child can try his hand at improvising an action-conversation monologue, a sequence of words and actions in which the role player pretends he is someone or something else and shares his thoughts with his listeners as if speaking confidentially to them. To stimulate children to think and to devise monologues, prepare index cards that contain a brief description of a possible situation such as:

- You are a package that holds cigarettes. Talk about your problems.
- You are a peel on a banana. What are your problems?
- You are a monkey looking out at the people who have come to look at *you* at the zoo. React to what you see.
- You are the football (or baseball) in a nationally televised game. How do you feel?
- You are a nut about to be cracked by a gigantic nutcracker. Tell how you feel as the cracker crumbles you.
- You are a cigar that is burning. It's hot! Talk about your problem.
- You are a garbage can, full and stinking! Talk about how you feel.
- You are the point on a very active pencil. Ouch! Describe your situation.
- You are a turkey on the day before Thanksgiving. How do you feel?
- You are an all-day sucker in the process of being devoured. Talk about your situation.

• You are an ant standing on a crowded elevator. Hey, watch your step there! Describe your situation.

Keep the situation cards in a small box in the listening-speaking corner of the classroom. List "Design an action-conversation monologue" as one of the options a child can select during independent study time. When the listening-speaking center is available, a child who selects the option can go to the corner, select a topic for his monologue from the suggested subjects, and role play the situation in the privacy of the listening center.

Make available a high stool so that a youngster who wants to try his hand at a monologue can climb up on the stool in the listening center, perch there, rest chin in hand, and talk with body and voice about how he—the nut, the banana peel, or the garbage can—feels. When a child feels comfortable with his monologue, he can sign up to share it with a small group of classmates or even with the entire class.

MORE ACTION-CONVERSATION MONOLOGUES
Ideas for monologues can come also from story books. A book in which the main character tells the story as if he or she were talking to the reader is ideal for this purpose. A youngster retells a part of the story pretending to be the main character and sharing his or her problems with those who listen. For example, Dr. Seuss' *And to Think That I Saw It on Mulberry Street* (Vanguard, 1937) is told by a young boy who imagines all manner of things that he sees on Mulberry Street but tells his father the truth—that he saw only a horse and wagon. A boy

in middle-elementary grades can pretend to be the character and explain his dilemma in monologue style to a group of listeners.

A different type of book is William Pene Du Bois's *Call Me Bandicott* (Harper, 1970). The central character in this book has a unique gift for getting money from other people. Bandicott's shrewdness as well as his stinginess provide material to build a monologue that has shades of humor.

Stories that have problem-type situations obviously are great for monologues. A good example of such a story is Evaline Ness' *Sam, Bangs and Moonshine* (Holt, 1966). Drawing her ideas from the Ness book, a girl can put together a monologue in which she confides about how her mendaciousness almost led to disaster. After reading E. L. Konigsburg's *About the B'nai Bagels* (Atheneum, 1969), a boy can pretend to be Mark and describe how impossible it is to have your mother manage your Little League team. Or remembering the situations in Armstrong Sperry's *Call It Courage* (Macmillan, 1940), a youngster can talk as if he is Mafatu, son of a Polynesian chieftain, and tell how he overcame fear in order to survive on the island of man eaters. A girl can do a similar interpretation of Karana, the young Indian girl who struggled for survival in the 1961 Newbery winner, Scott O'Dell's *Island of the Blue Dolphins* (Houghton Mifflin, 1960). As this brief paragraph implies, many of the books children love to read and reread can be sources of a monologue; children who have been introduced to the monologue may find this technique an enjoyable way of sharing books with others and at the same time gain skill in expressing thoughts verbally and nonverbally.

PICTURE ROLE PLAYING An emotion packed picture can motivate role playing. On cardboard mount pictures of several children interacting; magazines, newspapers, and even calendars are readily available sources of such stimuli.

Keep the pictures in a large box or in a file drawer. As an independent study activity, several youngsters can go to the picture file, select a picture, and improvise the actions and words that happened just before, during, and after the photograph was snapped. The youngsters can carry out the activity in the privacy of a listening-speaking center cordoned off from the rest of the class by a book case or screen or in the privacy of an adjacent hall. If participating youngsters request time, they can share their role playing sequence later on with classmates.

There are several commercial picture series designed particularly to stimulate verbal and nonverbal role playing activity. For example, Holt, Rinehart, and Winston produces, as part of its social science program *People in Action,* a number of pictures in flip-chart form that depict youngsters in emotional situations. One striking picture in the series shows several boys standing in front of the library, holding a badly torn book; their faces express fearful concern. Role playing such a situation can be listed as an option for an independent study activity, or can be designated as an activity for several youngsters to share during a predetermined period of time.

THE ELEVATOR GAME When people are packed closely together in an elevator, they tend to stare into space and not make eye contact with the strangers who stand close to them. They also tend to tense their body muscles so that the parts of the body that must touch strangers jammed on the elevator are not relaxed. To study this social phenomenon, which is related to the distances people like to maintain between themselves and others, mark off a square the size of an elevator in the corner of the classroom. One student becomes the elevator operator. Other children board the elevator in twos and threes as the elevator progresses upward. Of course, as more children enter the confined space, they will be thrown closer and closer together until their bodies are touching. Children can role play the situation pretending that the other people on the elevators are strangers, then pretending that they are friends.

There are several modifications of the elevator game that can be used with upper-elementary-grade youngsters. Children can role play being on a crowded, rapidly moving subway car, standing in line for a bus (how close does one stand to the person next in line?), or even shoving through a crowd. Again follow up with an interpretive activity in which children observe the distances people maintain between themselves and others in everyday situations and try to interpret the meanings sent by changes in distance.

SITUATIONAL ROLE PLAYING In certain social situations, persons tend to mask their true feelings and express themselves in ways that conflict with how they are actually feeling. Role playing can help older young people to see this social phenomenon in action.

Since masking of feelings occurs in the presence of another person, this role playing must involve at least two players. To facilitate role playing, print pairs of roles on index cards. Hand one of a pair to one player, the other to a second player. Each player, without preliminary consultation with the other, must come forward and express the thoughts and feelings described on the card he or she received. Obviously, each player sees only his or her own card, not the card of the other player.

Examples of situational descriptions are given below:

Card A, Giver: You are giving a birthday gift to a very good friend. You picked it out especially because you want to please her or him. You wrapped it yourself. Your fellow role player is that friend. Present your gift expressing the eagerness you feel.

Card B, Receiver: It is your birthday. Your best friend is giving you a gift. Express your immediate appreciation. Open it in such a way that you show your excitement. But when you open it, you find that you don't like it. Your friend is looking at you waiting for your expression of pleasure. React so as not to hurt him or her.

Card A, Teacher: You don't like the way a student has completed a piece of work. To you it looks like a shoddy piece of work and as if the student had just dashed it off. Tell the student and get across the idea that he better not do an assignment that way again.

Card B, Student: You are being bawled out by the teacher for doing a piece of sloppy work. The teacher implies that you dashed it off and requires that you do it again. Actually you spent a lot of time on that assignment, but you know that it pays to agree with this teacher. Play the role of the agreeing student who hides his own feelings to please the teacher, who does not appreciate disagreement.

Card A, Group members (make several of these cards):
You are a member of a group discussing going to an
amusement park to have a good time. You want to go
and express your pleasure at the idea. Play the role of
enthusiastic group member.

Card B, Newcomer to the group: Play the role of a newcomer who is unsure about how fellow members feel
about you. The group is discussing plans to go to an
amusement park; you don't want to go there because
it's a pretty rough place. But you're afraid to say so
for fear of making enemies. So you go along with
their plans against your better judgment.

After numbers of youngsters have played each
situation, divide the class into groups of five. Give
each group a copy of the following directions:

When We Cover Up Our Feelings

1. Very often we cover up what we are really feeling.
Try to recall when you have done this or seen another
person do this.

2. Prepare a chart listing examples given by group members. One group member should serve as scribe.

SITUATION IN WHICH FEELINGS WERE COVERED UP	WHY FEELINGS WERE COVERED UP
1.	
2.	
3.	
4.	

3. After at least five examples are listed, talk about why the person covering up his feelings felt he had to put on a "false face." List the reasons for covering up feelings in the right column.

4. When you have completed your chart, select one member to report your findings to the entire class. The reporter should be ready to explain reasons why people cover up their true feelings.

When each group has compiled a chart, post the charts around the room by hanging them on easels or pinning them to bulletin boards. Each group reporter comes to a central area in the classroom, sits facing the rest of the class, and explains what the items in the Why Feelings Were Covered Up column mean. When all have reported, encourage youngsters to generalize.

An interpretive activity of the types described in Chapter 6 can follow. Youngsters can be on the look out for covering up behavior of people outside the classroom. As they uncover such behavior, they can describe the incident briefly on a chart posted in the classroom and hypothesize with classmates as to why the person was covering up his feelings. Of course, a related question is how the observer knew that the person was covering up his true feelings and putting a false expression on his face. Generally nonverbal clues give the masker away, and the observer notes some inconsistency between what the person is saying with words and what the person is saying with physical expression. When children get to this sophisticated stage of looking for contradictory clues, a third column can be added to their charts, and they can draw further conclusions about the meaning of nonverbal activity in communication.

Situation in Which Feelings Were Covered Up	Why Feelings Were Covered Up	Clues That Gave the True Message

SUMMARY THOUGHTS

As the general structure of activities described in Chapters 2 and 3 imply, designing activities to teach nonverbal communication skills does not differ radically from designing typical activities in the elementary school curriculum. Nor is it necessary to teach these skills outside the context of instruction in the more traditional language arts areas—listening, speaking, reading, and writing.

In designing nonverbally oriented experiences, the teacher often can restructure activities already in the curriculum, such as pantomiming and dramatic activities, so that the stress is not just on words but on nonverbal expression as well. Then, too, some nonverbal experiences can be integrated into lessons or individualized learning experiences that focus on overall language development. Non-

verbal activity can be a jump-off into poetry, play,
or story writing, into listening and speaking experiences, and into encounters with language and literature. Conversely, these other language experiences
can be a jump-off into nonverbal expression. In this
context, children may come to see nonverbal language as a dimension of a larger whole—communication.

IV: you are on stage

While reading or telling stories, poems, jokes, and riddles to other children, youngsters, especially those in the upper grades, can become intimately involved in the pivotal elements of nonverbal communication. Faced with the task of making a story or poem interesting to listeners, the teller or reader must try out different vocal techniques and develop ways of using his body to heighten the effects of the spoken words.

The teller or reader must think about how to position his body: will sitting, standing, or leaning be best for a particular story or joke and with this particular audience? The interpreter must think about elements within the story that can be used to raise the audience's interest level: what props can be used to heighten the effect? The teller must study the riddle or joke to determine the places to pause just momentarily to add suspense, the places to raise the pitch of his voice to get attention, and the tone of voice to use for the different characters. He must decide how his voice can be manipulated to add to the verbal message. In considering these and other related questions, the teller of stories, poems, jokes, and riddles encounters elements of nonverbal language.

Of course, in planning how he is going to share a story or poem, a teller does not practice each and every gesture before a mirror or predetermine each and every inflection of his voice. When sharing, the teller does not gesture artificially or use his voice in an unnatural way. Practicing means getting to know the story material so well that the teller or reader has a feel for the message—its peaks and low points, the feelings to be expressed, and the nature of the action. In short, the teller "climbs into the story, the poem, or the joke headfirst!" so that he can share it and all its changing moods.

As with other classroom activities, the oral interpretation of literature should not be an academic exercise. Youngsters should enjoy preparing material for reading or telling to a real audience—an audience for whom the stories or poems or jokes were written. Ideal material to use in elementary schools is the picture story book. A picture story written for primary grade children can be read to younger children by upper-elementary grade youngsters; such books are simple enough for an upper-grade youngster to interpret physically and vocally, and they appeal to younger children. Picture story books, too, have been written by professionals who know that their books will be read aloud. Therefore, the reader often finds:

> A natural rhythm to the words.
> Noises, sounds, and plenty of dialogue written into the story.
> Places in which it would be natural to pause.
> Variations in mood that can be reflected vocally.
> Situations that almost demand some physical interpretation as well as vocal variation.

Because picture story books have such a ready audience in the elementary grades and because in many cases the authors wrote the stories knowing the tales would be read aloud, most of the activities in this section—a section designed primarily as an aid to the upper-grade teacher—center on the picture story book as a source of material to be interpreted vocally and physically. Teachers will also find suggestions for using video- and audio-tape recordings to enhance children's encounters with nonverbal communication.

TELLING STORIES

WATCH THE EXPERTS To introduce upper-elementary school youngsters to storytelling activities and motivate them to try their hand at storyreading, a teacher can show a master storyteller in action. The "Bank Street Reading Incentive Films" (distributed by McGraw-Hill) are one source of master storytellers. Children can watch Bill Cosby on film interpret Bernard Waber's *Rich Cat, Poor Cat.* They can watch Cosby chase his tail when he becomes the cat, use his hands to simulate waving motion, and bang the garbage can to add visual and sound effects; they can listen to the way he manipulates his voice to heighten effects.

After the children and teacher have identified some of Cosby's storytelling techniques in *Rich Cat, Poor Cat,* show Harry Belafonte reading *Gilberto and the Wind* or any of the other films in the series. In groups, upper-grade youngsters can identify the techniques used and list them on large-sized paper.

In working with this activity, the teacher may find it worthwhile for children to view a film more than once. The first showing is for enjoyment; in later showings, children can focus on an analysis of the expert's nonverbal storytelling techniques.

LISTEN TO THE STARS   Teachers can also use phonograph records and tapes of well-known performers reading stories to develop children's awareness of the vocal characteristics important in effective storytelling. Caedmon Records brings children such stars as Carol Channing reading the *Madeline* stories and *Winnie-the-Pooh,* Claire Bloom reading *Goldilocks and the Three Bears* and other fairy tales, and Vincent Price reading *Tales of Witches, Ghosts, and Goblins.*

After listening once to a recording to become familiar with the story, children listen a second time to identify vocal techniques of the reader; they jot down places in which the reader came across most effectively. After the second listening session, they can work in groups to summarize what they noticed during the listening period. It probably is helpful for the children to have copies of the story in front of them as they work in groups. As they talk about the ways in which the storyteller manipulated his voice, individual children can try out some of the same storytelling effects.

Weston Woods and Miller-Brody sound filmstrips and films can be used in a similar activity. Children look at the film and listen to the sound track during the first showing; during the second run-through, they listen only to the sound track without pictures. Again children follow up their listening activity with group discussion of effects noted and try out some of the techniques themselves.

TELLING STORIES IN WHICH SOUND IS IMPORTANT   Try a story analysis with older children.

First, read in a monotone a story such as Margaret Wise Brown's *Shhhhhh Bang* (Harper & Row, 1943), the story of a quiet, sleeping town in which even the train conductor whispers and of a boy who decides to wake up the place. After hearing the expressionless reading of the story, the children can discuss the tone and loudness of voice to be used in reading the quiet and noisy parts of the story; they can decide what noise-making props they could use in their own oral interpretation. Then individually or in groups they can prepare to read it to younger children. If the activity is carried out in groups, one child from each group is chosen by lot to read the story to children in a lower grade.

Other stories with built-in noise effects that older children can interpret vocally and nonverbally include: the noisy books by Margaret Wise Brown—*The Indoor Noisy Book* (1942), *Noisy Book City* (1939), and *Winter Noisy Book* (1947; all Harper & Row), Karla Kuskin's *All Sizes of Noises* (Harper & Row, 1962), Ezra Jack Keats' *Whistle for Willie* (Viking, 1964), and Lou Ann Gaeddert's *Noisy Nancy and Nick* (Doubleday, 1970).

Two more books written for younger children that older youngsters can use to gain skill in interpreting sounds are Peter Spier's *Crash! Bang! Boom!* (Doubleday, 1972) and *Gobble, Growl, Grunt* (Doubleday, 1971). These books are full of sound words. *Gobble, Growl, Grunt* juxtaposes the sounds made by animals with pictures of those animals; *Crash! Bang! Boom!* is filled with pictures of machines and the sounds they make—rrrassp-rassp, boom-hum-boomboom, hustle, bing-bong. An upper-grade youngster can select just a page from one of these books and try out renditions of the sound effects. Several youngsters can share several pages with which they have experimented with kindergarten children. As a matter of fact, they can even try pantomiming the actions of the animals or machines for the younger children. A follow-up can be a written activity in which children write stories that contain phonetic representations of the sounds found in a Peter Spier's book.

A similar experience can be built around Janet Wolff's *Let's Imagine Sounds* (Dutton, 1962). Ssshhh, bang, plop, and zoom are just a few of the sounds in this book in which half the pages are upside-down. Again individuals or small groups of upper-grade youngsters can prepare to read the book to little children.

And then there are books like Theodor Storm's *Little John* (Farrar, Straus and Giroux, 1972) that are chock-full of words to be called out, roared, whispered, and crowed. Little John shouts, the sun roars, and the crow says, "Kiii-ker-ri-kiiiiii," all of which an older youngster can utter when he shares the story with K-2ers.

STORIES IN WHICH GESTURES HAVE A PLACE
Try another story analysis with older children. Read in a monotone and without gesture or a change in facial expression a story in which some words or actions almost cry out to be expressed through gestures or pantomime. Bemelman's *Madeline's Rescue* (Viking, 1953) is a good example. There are turning out the light, slipping and falling, climbing on a stool

to protest, and searching high and low. After hearing the story read without expression, children can decide how these and other actions can best be "told." Refer back to the interpretation of sounds in the preceding activity and ask the children to think about how to speak the "tap, tap, tap" in the Madeline adventure. Refer to previous considerations of loudness when children try out different ways of speaking Madeline's protest to Lord Cucuface.

Again individually or in groups children can try interpreting parts of the story and prepare to read it to younger children. With a book as lengthy as *Madeline's Rescue,* group activity may actually be more productive than a solo endeavor. Each member of a storytelling team prepares a portion of the story and reads that portion to smaller children as the story proceeds.

Other stories in which gestures have a logical role and do not appear affected when introduced into storytelling include:

Frank Herrmann's *The Giant Alexander and Hannibal the Elephant* (McGraw-Hill, 1972). An elephant gets stuck on the railroad track; everyone pushes, pulls, heaves, and shoves with no success. Then Alexander rubs the elephant's foot with butter, freeing the beast to go on to further adventures. The story is loaded with action words that can be expressed nonverbally.

Yoshiko Samuel's *Twelve Years, Twelve Animals* (Abingdon Press, 1972). This story begins: "Long time ago in Japan, King decided to invite all the animals. . ." Some of the animals invited are a tiger, a dragon, and a rabbit. Their actions as they prepare to visit the King can be pantomimed by the storyteller.

William Steig's *Amos and Boris* (Farrar, Straus and Giroux, 1971). The blossoming friendship between a mouse and a whale is related. A storyteller can push, rock to-and-fro as if on a boat, roll, dive, splash, swim, and so on.

Polly Greenberg's *Oh Lord, I Wish I Was a Buzzard* (Macmillan, 1968). A little girl who must pick and pick and pick and pick cotton, wishes she were a dog "going huh-huh-huh," a buzzard "going round and round in the sky," a snake "curled up cold and cool," and a butterfly "bouncing from blossom to blossom." A storyteller can show as well as tell about these actions.

TELLING STORIES WITH VARYING EMOTIONS

Children can experiment with expressing different emotions with the voice by telling stories in which feeling and mood are essential ingredients or in which a wide range of emotions is expressed. An example is Eth Clifford's *A Bear Before Breakfast* (Putnam, 1962) in which two youngsters experience excited anticipation followed by understanding and dejection as they discover that they have misunderstood what they have been told. Read without expression a story such as this to older-elementary school children. Ask them to decide in groups how the story should be read. Give each group an episode to interpret by trying out different ways of speaking the lines. After a short period of group experimenting, each group selects a storyteller, and each in turn interprets for the class.

Other books useful for developing vocal expressiveness include May Garelick's *Where Does the Butterfly Go When It Rains?* (William R. Scott, 1961), Alice Goudey's *The Day We Saw the Sun Come Up*

(Scribners, 1961), and Uri Shulevitz's *One Monday Morning* (Scribners, 1967) and *The Moon in My Room* (Harper & Row, 1963).

WATCH YOUR RATE   Divide an upper-elementary class into three-person teams and distribute to each group a picture story book and a card that asks:

- Where could you pause in telling this story to add suspense or build audience anticipation?
- Where could you read quickly or slow down to make your oral interpretation reflect the meaning and pace of the story?

A three-person team studies a story and tries pausing at different places and reading at different rates. When they have prepared and practiced their reading, one youngster from each group goes to the first grade to read the story to three children. The upper-grade teams can try the activity on several occasions using other books so that each youngster on a telling team gets a chance to interpret a story for younger children.

Stories that serve especially well for this purpose include Beatrice de Regniers' *May I Bring a Friend?* (Atheneum, 1964) and Leo Lionni's *Frederick* (Pantheon, 1967).

STORYTELLING TO MUSIC   Stories related to musical selections are particularly well suited for oral interpretation. Youngsters can listen to a recording of the musical presentation of a story and can even prepare an abbreviated version of the music by taping appropriate portions. The tapes can serve as a background for story sharing.

There are numerous books that relate stories based on musical classics. For example, Alfred A. Knopf has published a picture story version of Sergei Prokofiev's *Peter and the Wolf;* a youngster who chooses to share that story can tell about Peter, the bird, and the cat to the musical accompaniment of the Prokofiev piece.

A new series published by Gakken Co. of Tokyo is also fine for sharing. Titles in this Fantasia Pictorial Series, all of which have their origins in musical classics, include:

G. A. Rossini's *William Tell,* illustrated by Hiroshi Mizusawa and adapted by Tamao Fujita (1971). William Tell's fight against evil which is personified by the governor of the province.

P. I. Tchaikovsky's *The Nutcracker,* illustrated by Fumiko Hori and adapted by Magoichi Kushida (1971). Marie's dream adventure with the nutcracker prince.

E. H. Grieg's *Peer Gynt,* illustrated by Yoshiharii Suzuki and adapted by Makoto Oishi (1971). The good-for-nothing's adventures as he seeks his fortune.

Saint-Saens' *Carnival of the Animals,* illustrated by Kozo Kakimoto and adapted by Keisuke Tsutsui (1971). An encounter with lions, elephants, swans, and a little old man.

D. B. Kabalevsky's *Joey the Clown (The Comedians)* illustrated by Saburo Watanabe and adapted by Keisuke Tsutsui (1971). Joey the Clown's antics include pulling cards and cards and cards from his shirt, skating on all fours, and throwing muffins in the air—all to try to get one little boy to laugh.

The books in the series are distributed in the United States by Silver Burdette. Recordings of the related musical selections can be obtained through any large record shop.

A similar type of story-sharing experience can be based on picture books that have songs accompanying the stories. The well-known classic in this category is John Langstaff's and Feodor Rojankovsky's Caldecott award-winning version of *Frog Went A-Courtin'* (Harcourt, Brace, 1955). There is a delightful little melody in the book to which each of the verses can be sung. Several youngsters can learn the song and share the story and pictures with smaller children as they sing. Or the youngsters can make a tape of the story-song, which later can be shared with classmates.

Other books that have the same possibilities for sharing by singing include:

Barbara Emberley's *One Wide River to Cross* (Prentice-Hall, 1966). The tale of Noah, the building of the ark, and the animals.

Glen Round's version of *Casey Jones: The Story of a Brave Engineer* (Golden Gate Junior Books, 1968). The ballad of Casey Jones, the mighty engineer who manned his post through thick and thin.

Osmond Molarsky's *The Song of the Empty Bottles* (Walck, 1968). The story of a boy who collects bottles and finds that he can play a tune with them.

Sorche Nic Leodhas's *Always Room for One More* (Holt, Rinehart and Winston, 1965). The story of Lachie MacLachlan in whose home all were welcome.

STORYTELLING WITH A FLANNEL BOARD Older
children can learn to manipulate flannel board
pieces to help communicate story action to a
younger listener. For instance, to tell Leo Lionni's
story of *Swimmy* (Pantheon, 1963), a youngster can
cut out of flannel a little black fish, a school of red
fish, and a big tuna fish. He can also make flannel
cut-outs of the other organisms inhabiting the sea
or cut out magazine pictures of them, and staple
sandpaper to the back to make them adhere to a
flannel board. Then as he relates Swimmy's adventures, he moves Swimmy across the flannel board
amid the flannel pieces representing the lobster, the
seaweed, and other sea life. This activity forces the
storyteller to use his hands to communicate the
story.

There are numbers of stories that can be told
effectively using the flannel board. Children can
select from: Marcia Brown's *The Three Billy Goats
Gruff* (Harcourt, Brace and Jovanovich, 1957), Leo
Lionni's *Theodore and the Talking Mushroom* (Pan-
theon, 1971), Violet Salazar's *Squares Are Not Bad!*
(Golden Press, 1967), Nonny Hogrogian's *One Fine
Day* (Macmillan, 1971), Edward Fenton's *The Big
Yellow Balloon* (Doubleday, 1967), Marie Hall Ets'
Play with Me (Viking, 1955), or Leo Lionni's *Little
Blue and Little Yellow* (Ivan Obolensky, 1959).

DRAWING STORIES In a drawing story the narrator illustrates line-by-line as he tells a story, generally
from memory. A classic drawing story is the tale of
a little boy who builds a house with doors, windows,
and chimneys, and then sets out to visit his friend

Sally. Sally takes a walk with the boy, climbing down cellar stairs, crawling through trap doors, slipping, falling, and getting up until they arrive back at the boy's house. The narrator tells the story action by drawing lines; the finished drawing resembles a cat. If you don't know the story, get Carl Withers' version, *The Tale of a Black Cat* (Holt, Rinehart and Winston, 1966). Tell and illustrate the story for youngsters. Then encourage children to invent original versions of the tale to share with classmates.

As a continuing adventure in storytelling, youngsters can start from scratch and invent their own tales for telling and drawing. Possible titles for story building are: "The Goat's Trip," "The Seagull Mystery," "A Snail's Pace," "The Turtle's Trip," "The Hungry Hound," "The Lost Hippopotamus," "The Camel's Hump," and "The Whale's Voyage."

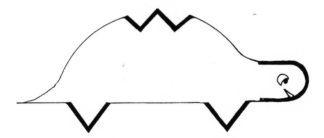

The "Turtle's Trip" is composed of two small V's, a small W, and a lazy U. Stories can be made up about the twins, Vance and Vick, their friend Walt, and their other friend, tired Ulysses. Youngsters who devise stories can share them with classmates and draw their turtle step by step.

SELECTING STORIES TO BE READ OR TOLD

After youngsters have had several encounters with

storytelling, take them to the library to select books for future oral reading. When they return to the classroom, they can talk about the reasons why they selected a particular book. Following their discussion, they can propose criteria for selecting books for storyreading. These criteria may include some of the following points:

- Are there concrete action words such as bounced, zoomed, or ripped that can be interpreted physically?
- Are there words that have a sound related to the meaning that can be used as part of the storytelling?
- Are there places where pauses can build anticipation or suspense?
- Are there differences in story mood that can be reflected in the voice through changes in loudness, pitch, or rate of reading?
- Are there changes in story mood that can be reflected through changes in facial expression?
- Are there places in the story that lend themselves to pantomiming?
- Are there places in the story or poem where actual things can be used as props?

These questions can serve as a selection guide during the next trip to the library to choose storytelling books.

VOCAL TAPING When individual children bring to the classroom books for oral or nonverbal interpretation, encourage them to try out different vocal effects and to record their interpretations on audiotape. This activity can be listed as an option among "Things to Do" during independent study sessions.

Create a listening-speaking center in the classroom simply by placing a bookcase perpendicular to

the wall and placing a cassette tape recorder on a
table positioned in the cubicle. Mount a mirror over
the table so that a youngster who wants to watch his
accompanying facial expressions can do so.

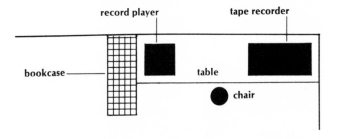

A CLASSROOM LISTENING-SPEAKING CENTER

An individual youngster can go to the center to
record his interpretations of a story and then listen
to the results in playback. He can ask a friend to
join him and help him decide which interpretation
of the several he has recorded is most effective and
should be used when sharing the story with younger
children.

Have a record player and a file of classical and
popular records available so that children can select
a record to serve as a musical background for their
storyreading. For instance, a youngster might read
Dr. Seuss' *And To Think That I Saw It on Mulberry
Street* (Vanguard, 1937) to the accompaniment of
"Seventy-six Trombones" or Barbara Emberley's
Drummer Hoff (Prentice-Hall, 1967) to the accompaniment of *The 1812 Overture*.

VIDEO-TAPING   In schools with video-taping equipment, an upper-grade youngster can practice reading

a story and then share it with classmates as the video-tape camera records his or her reading. If children are video-taped, after they have had several experiences with storytelling and reading, they may develop a checklist of questions to be considered during play-back:

* Did I read too quickly?
* Did I make eye contact with my audience?
* Did I lean toward or away from my audience to vary my contact with my listeners?
* Did I use gestures for emphasis?

As children view their own video-tapes, they may be able to identify additional items related to voice and body control. Sometimes the development of such a checklist after numerous storytelling/reading opportunities serves as a summarizing activity; youngsters must learn to verbalize their growing understandings about the intricacies of nonverbal communication.

Playback of video-tapes should be an individual activity with the storyteller viewing his own tape in the privacy of the recording booth. Only if he expresses the desire, should the tape be shared with others, and then as a listening activity devoid of analytical criticism by the listeners. Some children enjoy sharing their tapes with small groups of children in lower grades.

GOING BEYOND STORIES

PLAYING WITH NURSERY RHYMES Telling a nursery rhyme is one way children can involve their entire bodies in communicating a message; to tell a rhyme almost demands a complete acting out of the physical activity of the rhyme. Divide the class into presentation groups comprised of three youngsters. Give each group a card bearing a rhyme—Little Jack Horner, Little Miss Muffet, Jack Be Nimble, Humpty Dumpty, Ride a Cock Horse to Banbury Cross, or one of the less well-known ones.

The groups decide how they can act out in unison the action as they tell the rhyme to smaller children. When each group has practiced, has located props to help in the telling, and has some notion of what they want to do with their rhyme, schedule a dress rehearsal for the class. Then "take the show on the road!" Go to the kindergartens and first grades of the school. The younger children can be clustered in the center of the room while the older children stand or sit in their groups around the perimeter of the room. Now it is Show Time, and each group performs.

If the upper-grade children like the idea, try participatory theatre. Repeat the show, but this time the young children—orally and nonverbally—join in. They, too, become Humpty Dumpty or Little Miss Muffet and have a firsthand, active encounter with expressive communication.

PLAYING WITH POEMS   Poems are meant to be heard. Sounds collide, echo, and re-echo, and silence is pregnant with meaning as a poem is read aloud. To read a poem to someone else is to play with sounds and with silence.

There are hundreds of poems that are just waiting to be read by children to other children. One splendid little volume for sharing is Leonard Doob's *A*

Crocodile Has Me by the Leg: African Poems (Walker and Co., 1966). A vibrant beat rings through Doob's poems, a rhythm that can be sounded on a drum by a youngster reading to another child or can be reflected in a pulsating motion of the reader's body.

Mary O'Neill's *What Is That Sound?* (Atheneum, 1966) abounds with poems such as "Baa?" "Growl?" and "What Is the Sound of Love?" that are perfect for oral interpretation. Eve Merriam's *Catch a Little Rhyme* (Atheneum, 1966) contains poems that two or three youngsters can select and prepare for a co-operative reading with each youngster interpreting several lines. If poem-sharers don't want to be physically encumbered by holding the book, they can prepare large cue cards; the cards can be propped on an easel and flipped by a team member during the poetry-sharing time.

Longer narrative poems can also be "performed" in this fashion by several youngsters working together on vocal and physical effects. Longfellow's "The Skeleton in Armor" and Thayer's "Casey at the Bat" serve well for this purpose. See Prentice-Hall's large picture book versions of these poems; the pictures with their pinch of humor can stimulate a non-verbal interpretation. Good too are action-sound poems such as Carl Cramer's *The Boy Drummer of Vincennes* (Harvey House, 1972), a poem based on George Rogers Clarke's march across Illinois to regain Vincennes. The boom, boom, boom, boom of the young drummer's drum echoes through the poem. A youngster who drums can supply a rhythmic background for the poem as it is interpreted orally by his or her classmate.

RIDDLES   Riddles were made for sharing; they also seem to have been made for children who enjoy one-up-manship by asking a riddle that is beyond solution. To tell a riddle with style requires considerable vocal control—the right tone, the appropriate pacing, and emphasis placed on just the right words. Riddles, therefore, are great for practicing vocal communication.

Keep several books of riddles in the classroom and encourage children to listen to and read them. When a youngster picks a riddle, he can first try it out in the listening-speaking center, and then see if he can stump his classmates or younger children. Here are a few titles of riddle books to select from: Maria Leach's *Riddle Me, Riddle Me, Ree* (Viking, 1970), Lillian Morrison's *Black Within and Red Without: A Book of Riddles* (Thomas Crowell, 1953), and William Wiesner's *A Pocketful of Riddles* (E. P. Dutton, 1966). These books are appropriate for use in upper-elementary grades.

IT'S A JOKE!   Joke telling also requires artful use of pause, changes in vocal inflection and rate of speaking, and a precise correlation of body expression with the verbal message. Since upper-elementary grade children are developing a sense of humor and enjoy jokes, telling jokes can be a fun way for children to encounter and try out some of the nonverbal aspects of communication.

Have available in the classroom some gag and joke books; alert children to listen for jokes on TV. When a child has heard or read a joke that appeals to his sense of humor, encourage him to try telling it in the recording center and listening to himself in playback until he has the joke under control. At the end of a dreary day, ask for volunteers who are ready to tell a joke.

After numbers of children have shared jokes, try producing a "Laugh-in" special. Jokers can use tables, boxes, or chairs as perches from which to tell their jokes in rapid fire progression a *la* "Laugh In." To add to the action, all the jokers can hold colored cardboard in front of their faces when they are not telling a joke. They pop out from behind their cardboards at the exact moment when they begin to tell their jokes. This type of activity can be interspersed with humorous skits such as those suggested in Chapter 2, on pages 51–2.

Joke books that you may wish to include in your classroom library include:

Oscar Weigle's *The Joke Book* (Grosset and Dunlap, 1963). An illustrated joke book for youngsters in grades four to six; lots of two-person jokes that two youngsters can select, prepare, and share as a team.

Marguerite Kohl and Frederica Young's *Jokes for Children* (Hill and Wang, 1963). Rhymes, puns, jokes; some great ones about teachers that children would have fun with.

Sonny Fox's *Jokes . . . and How to Tell Them* (Putnam, 1965). Monster jokes, sallies, and knock-knocks with some advice from a master on how to tell them.

As with the riddle books, the joke books listed are most appropriately used with upper graders.

MAGIC A magic show is a fun way to involve youngsters simultaneously in nonverbal and verbal language, for the magician must keep up a running patter as he shows, handles, points, and mystifies.

Have magic books available on the bookshelf where you keep your riddle and joke books. As a group activity, youngsters can practice magic acts they read about in such books as:

Robert Lopshire's *It's Magic?* (London: Collier-Macmillan Ltd., 1969). Magic for the little ones, K-2.

Francis Rigney's *A Beginner's Book of Magic* (Devin-Adair Co., 1964). Magic for youngsters in the middle grades.

Ib Permin's *Hokus Pokus* (Sterling Publishing Co., 1969). Magic for grades 6-9.

WRITE YOUR OWN TO SHARE   As children interpret vocally and physically the picture books, poems, and jokes written by professionals, they intuitively gain an understanding of how such written pieces are put together. For instance, they sense that repetition of sounds, words, phrases, and even sequences of events can add to a story when it is read aloud; they see the value of dialogue in a story as they vary their voices to become the little bear, the middle-sized bear, and the big bear; and they begin to perceive that anticipation can be built up by the pause necessary to turn a page and that words are placed on a page to capitalize on that effect.

Having read published stories to little children, older children can begin to write stories of their own for oral presentation. A youngster can work alone or on a team, writing and illustrating an original story. The illustrations and text can be stapled or glued to sheets and bound together in book form. The child or the writing-illustrating team practices reading the story using all the techniques related to control of voice and body learned when reading published books. If the book is a team project, team members together work out techniques for orally interpreting their story. Each goes to a different class to share the story with younger children.

In the same manner, children can build their own books of poems, jokes, riddles, and magic either individually or cooperatively and share their original material with youngsters in lower grades.

SUMMARY THOUGHTS

Some attention is now being given to the advantages accruing from older children serving as teachers for younger children. An article in the February 5, 1973, issue of *Newsweek* highlights the growing awareness:

In the days of the one-room schoolhouse, older pupils often had to help teach the younger children. Schools have become a lot more elaborate since then, but now modern educators are relearning an old lesson: younger children thrive when they are taught by older students, and the older pupils often benefit from playing teacher.

One benefit that comes from serving as teacher is the opportunity to use both verbal and nonverbal language creatively to convey meanings to others. That benefit is clearly apparent when youngsters interpret stories, poems, and jokes orally for little children. The older storyteller must use gestures effectively, must express feelings vocally and physically, and must vary his speed and loudness of voice if he is to get the little ones involved in the story. Then, too, the storyteller gets immediate feedback through the eyes and facial expressions of his listeners; he learns to "listen" to the nonverbal feedback of his listeners and to speed up or slow down to hold their attention. And, of course, the storyteller gains self-confidence; he learns to handle himself in front of an audience, which—because of the age difference—is essentially unthreatening to him.

V: LET'S
JUST TALK

It is possible to design activities into the curriculum that call for nonverbal expression as part of the give-and-take of normal conversation. Particularly appropriate are conversations in which a participant must handle and show concrete materials or must refer to items by pointing. Also appropriate are conversations in which one person is really excited, in which one person wants to convince another, or in which participants discuss topics or ideas that can be expressed with hand motions, such as describing a spiral staircase or a sequence of events.

It is also possible to devise contrived activities that lead to general conclusions about the nature of nonverbal language—about the way body language, vocal language, and the manipulation of time, space, objects, and people affect others' impressions of a situation.

Chapter 5 focuses on both contrived and general discussion-type activities. Of course, because conversation is the basis of all the activities described, verbal as well as nonverbal skills are involved.

CONVERSATIONAL ACTIVITIES

LOOK HERE!—INDICATING BY SHOWING To clarify, a speaker may point or gesture toward an object about which he is talking. Map or globe study is ideal for encouraging such gestures that clarify. Keep a pointer in readiness. Ask children to come to the map and use the pointer to indicate the city, ocean, mountain, or state being discussed or to indicate the direction of river flow or the movement of air masses. Students can similarly clarify by pointing to locations on the globe, by rotating the globe on its axis to explain day and night, and by walking with the globe to show the earth's revolution around the sun.

Whenever pictures, charts, or diagrams are projected on a screen whether via overhead, slide, or filmstrip projector, students can clarify explanations of these visuals nonverbally. In a picture in which smoke or trees are being blown by the wind, students can indicate wind direction through gestures; in a picture in which shadows are evident, students can indicate the probable location of the sun by pointing; and in a picture of a wooded area in winter, students can indicate signs of animal life by showing. On a projected chart, students can point to specific items that relate to an idea being discussed; they can point in sequential order to items to answer a "What happened first? second? third?" question. With a diagram, students can identify key components or can show direction of flow or action by pointing.

A special caution! Some teachers ask a question, wait for a verbal response, and then translate nonverbally by pointing to the map, chart, picture, globe, or diagram. Perhaps the statement made initially bears repeating. Keep a pointer in readiness. When you ask a question that requires a student to indicate a location or a direction of action, hand the pointer to the respondent, suggesting nonverbally that he answer by showing. You move out of the center-front position so that clarification through nonverbal expression becomes a student responsibility.

LOOK HERE!—FOCUSING ATTENTION   A technique, suggested throughout this book, for small group recording of findings is the large chart made with a flow pen. This technique provides a simple way for groups to summarize discussion ideas; it also provides a visual means of sharing ideas during the reporting period that follows small group discussion. In addition, it almost forces a reporter to focus attention by pointing. Armed with a pointer, the reporter gestures toward items listed on the group chart as he discusses each item.

A TALK BOX   A talk box is simply a medium-sized box covered with colored paper. A picture that holds some special appeal for the children in the class is mounted on each side of the box. A child takes the box and selects a picture from the six mounted on it. He then talks about what the picture says to him, sharing his thoughts with other youngsters in the class or in his small talk group.

Interestingly enough, holding a talk box in their hands is great for youngsters who fidget when sharing ideas with others. The box keeps their hands occupied and becomes something to show and gesture toward.

A DISCUSSION WALK   A walk to locate specific objects can trigger pointing gestures and follow-up discussion on the appropriateness of pointing. Just a few of the things youngsters can look for, point out, and record data on are:

- Signs of man's carelessness.
- Buildings in need of repair.

- Trees of one kind, e.g., all the maples, all the pines, all the oaks, all the spruces, all the ginkos, or all the dog-woods.
- Signs of man's attempt to beautify his environment.
- Signs of animal life other than man.
- Vehicles with polluting exhausts.
- Vehicles making loud noises.

Back in the classroom, children talk about the things they saw and why it is considered polite to point at these things and not polite to point at people in the same way.

SHOW US—TELLING ABOUT BY SHOWING   A person talking about something he is holding in his hand is very likely to vary the position of the object to display it and to gesture toward the object as he talks. To help children acquire skill in telling about by showing, set aside time for youngsters to share some well-liked object or animal friend with fellow students. Keep a Show Us! sign-up chart posted on the coming events section of the bulletin board; the chart can list future times when youngsters will tell by showing:

Show Us!	**SELECT A TIME**
	Tuesday 10:05 _____
	Wednesday 2:00 _____
	Friday 2:30 _____

GRAB A THING   Keep a grab bag in the classroom so that a youngster can grab an object and describe it to classmates. As in the preceding activity, just holding an object about which one is talking encourages pointing and displaying gestures. Here are kinds of objects to throw into the grab bag:

feather	old bus ticket
foreign coin	medal
nutcracker	whistle
suit label	used airline ticket
empty shell	crab claw
empty book of matches	wrapper from a can of
pencil with an inscription	chocolate-covered ants

Keep the grab bag by the door. When children line up and there is a moment to spare, the child first in line "grabs a thing" and describes it on-the-spot to his classmates.

YOU WOULDN'T BELIEVE WHAT HAPPENED TO ME! In telling about something exciting that happened, a person may use facial expressions and gestures to convey not only the sense of what actually happened but also a sense of how he felt—fear, anger, concern, or pleasure. A bulletin board captioned You Wouldn't Believe What Happened To Me! serves as kick-off into sessions in which youngsters describe an exciting event. To the board add such subcaptions as:

I was scared stiff	Out in the storm
Did I hate her	It was a dandy day
What I overheard	Witness to disaster
The game we won	Time to go home
The game we lost	A race to the end
Fun in the amusement park	Nice things do happen
A wonderful ride	We had to find a solution
Stuck	Mystery

During independent study periods children select titles from the board (or make up their own) and write stories or tell stories into the tape recorder describing an exciting happening. When several children have prepared written or taped drafts of stories, schedule a story sharing time. With everyone sitting on the floor, legs crossed informal style, story sharers retell their stories from memory. Listeners ask questions to elicit more details, and perhaps spontaneously a listener will talk about a similar exciting incident that happened to him or her.

WHEN EXCITEMENT MOUNTS Encourage spontaneous talk about exciting things. During independent study times youngsters can form talk pairs. Two youngsters who want to talk about an exciting happening move into the listening-speaking corner to converse. To introduce youngsters who are accustomed to more traditional seat work to this more active use of independent study, list "talk pairs" as an option from which youngsters can select.

At first you may have to be specific to get children involved in talk pairs. The talk option may read:

- Did you see the World Series game? Find a conversation mate, go to the listening-speaking center, and describe the final inning.

- Did you see the adventures in Africa program on TV last night? Find a conversation mate to discuss it with.

- Did you read about the explosion at the electric plant? Find a conversation mate, go to the listening-speaking center, and tell him about it.

How To!—Giving Directions   In giving directions, a speaker may point to focus attention and/or perform a series of motions that show in concrete fashion how to do something. For example, in describing how to strike a match, the direction-giver may show in pantomime how to hold the book of matches and strike away from the body.

On long strips of paper print suggested directions for students to give. The directions may be those necessary for carrying out simple procedures such as:

How to strike a match	How to bisect an angle
How to swim a certain stroke (the crawl, the breast stroke)	How to catch a fly
	How to hold a baseball bat and hit a ball
How to paddle a canoe	How to play hopscotch
How to mount a horse	How to play volleyball
How to balance on a skate or surf board	How to serve in tennis
	How to play stickball
How to hit a golf ball	How to ice skate

Or the directions may be how to get from one place to another in the local community, how to get from:

> The school to the municipal building
> The bus station to your house
> The library to your house

Put the direction strips into a large envelope or string them across the entrance to the listening-speaking corner. Preparing directions can be an option youngsters can select during independent study time; in pairs they can select a direction strip, go to the listening-speaking center, and practice giving directions to one another. Of course, practice implies trying out both words and gestures as the direction-giving pair communicate with one another.

LISTEN, WATCH, AND DO—GIVING MORE DIRECTIONS Youngsters pair off into two-person teams. One—the doer—is given paper and pencil and turns his back to the chalkboard. The other—the teller—watches as the teacher draws on the board a shape such as any of those shown below.

Shapes to Use for Listen, Watch, and Do. Start Drawing at the Point Indicated by the Big Dot.

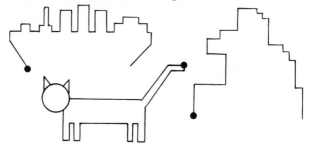

After the teacher has drawn the shape, the doer, back still to the board, takes pencil in hand. The teller must now give him directions using words and actions to get the doer to reproduce the shape on paper. For instance, the teller may say, "Draw a line a short distance upward"; simultaneously he holds up his fingers to indicate length and direction of line. The only thing the teller *cannot* say is what the shape looks like, e.g., he cannot say, "The shape is a boat."

To give children some preparatory background for this activity, the teacher may want to draw a shape on the board for all to see. Several children can give how-to-draw sentences and simultaneously explain how through nonverbal expression.

Listen, Watch, and Do can be played a number of times with tellers and doers switching positions so that everyone has the opportunity to express and interpret messages. At each playing, of course, a new drawing must be used. After an initial playing, individual children can take over the teacher's task of drawing additional shapes for students to describe and reproduce.

DESCRIBING   In classroom talk sessions, be alert for opportunities for children to use nonverbal expression as part of their talk about things around them. Discussion touching upon action things such as merry-go-rounds, cranes, pneumatic drills, animals, airplanes, chairs that swivel, or subways, or about activities such as rowing, throwing, pounding, creeping, pushing, scraping, knocking, or slipping is great for stimulating gestures and body motions that describe actions. As children talk, look for the teachable moment to suggest, "Yes, and *show* me!"

COMPARING AND CONTRASTING   In comparing or contrasting two things, a speaker may gesture with his left hand as he refers to one thing, and then with his right hand as he refers to the other. In addition, if the things are concrete objects, the speaker may use his hands to describe more explicitly the characteristics of the objects he is comparing and/or contrasting.

To help students gain skill in using nonverbal techniques to supplement verbal comparisons and contrasts, write on slips of paper the names of two related objects. The following related pairs serve as an easy introduction to nonverbal comparisons and contrasts:

cube	sphere
spoon	fork
frying pan	cooking pot
cactus	tulip
spiral staircase	regular staircase
leaf	flower
baseball	football
sieve	bowl
orange	banana
pine tree	maple tree

The class divides into five-person teams; each team member draws a slip of paper from a grab bag and extemporaneously tells his teammates the similarities and differences between the two related objects. Using just the ten items suggested above, each team can play twice. Then youngsters can think up other related word pairs to use for further team play during independent study periods.

CONVINCE ME   In convincing other people, a speaker gestures to emphasize, leans his body toward his listeners to add impact to his message, and moves his entire body as he becomes involved in what he is saying. Role-playing activities can introduce the verbal and nonverbal languages of persuasion and can lead to situations in which children try to convince others as they interact in the give-

and-take of classroom discussion. Ask for volunteers to improvise the following:

> Convince a sales person to let you return a nonreturnable item.
>
> Convince someone to buy a product you are selling.
>
> Convince someone to give up smoking.
>
> Convince someone to go to a horror movie with you—he doesn't like horror movies.
>
> Convince your mother or father that you need a new coat (dress, shirt, shoes).
>
> Convince a friend to drive slowly to conserve gasoline.
>
> Convince a teacher that you shouldn't have so much homework.

Between "plays," children talk about and show actions that role players are using. The role players —both the convincer and the person to be convinced—tell the reasons for what they said and did. Then other students play the same scene, experimenting with original gestures and facial expressions.

After youngsters have experienced a total class role playing period, Convince Me can be added to the list of options from which individuals can choose during independent study times. A youth selecting the option must decide on a topic that interests him. For example, during an election campaign, he might choose to persuade others to support his candidate, or he might choose to convince others of the necessity to support a particular course of action such as equal rights for women, improved pollution control, or more money for rapid transit. He may focus on conditions in the school and build an argument for relaxed rules in the hall, more time for athletics, or a different way to organize classroom activities. In the privacy of the listening-speaking center, he tries out actions and words. When he is ready, he signs up for class time to convince others.

WHICH IS FIRST?—ORDERING   When a person talks about events that existed or occurred in a particular sequential order, he makes a gesturing move with his hand as he mentions "first," "second," and then "third." In a sense, the hand gesture serves as a dividing marker—a nonverbal comma—setting off the items in the series and making meanings clearer.

To involve elementary-school youngsters in gestures that suggest serial order, set up conversations that require sequential thinking. Such conversations may be short interchanges built within the framework of a larger, ongoing discussion. In a reading lesson, for instance, ask youngsters to retell a sequence of story events: Ask, "Gwynn, what happened first? What happened second?"

In a group writing session in which youngsters are describing the events of a class trip for an experience story chart, ask, "What did we do first? second? third?" After students view a film, ask, "Will someone review the important events that happened in the film?" After students listen to a classroom report, ask, "What are the three points Jeff made? Can you tell them in order?"

Even as you watch for new words used by students in the give-and-take of discussion and build those words on the spot into the vocabulary of other students, watch for gestures that occur spontaneously in conversation. Turn these spontaneous gestures into firsthand examples of the way hand signals can clarify a communication.

Also since children learn much through imitation, when you describe work to be completed in a particular order, employ clear-cut gestures as you speak of what is to be done first, second, and last. Ask a student who needs practice in clear gesturing to repeat the directions in order. You may find that the student automatically imitates your gestures even as he uses the same words you spoke. A similar technique can be used when talking about the chronology of historical events or the steps in a laboratory experiment. When *you* talk of events or sequences, speak with nonverbal distinctness, gesturing sharply to set off items in the series. Then ask youngsters to explain a related series of events or steps.

Note: Such discussion activity has an added built-in bonus. Children are not only learning to handle nonverbal language, but they are also learning to work with an important cognitive process—sequential thinking.

IF. . . . THEN   A speaker may turn to gestures to clarify if–then relationships. When stating, "If peace comes, then we must work to rebuild what has been destroyed," the speaker marks the subordinate *if* clause with a gesture of the hand, and the main *then* clause with a parallel gesture of the other hand.

As with sequential ordering, the way to involve youngsters in nonverbal clarification of if–then relationships is first to build if–then thinking into discussions. In reading lessons, ask, "If you were

Tom, what would you do?" or "If Tom had done nothing, what would have happened?" In science experiences, query, "If we heat solid sulfur, what will happen? If we cool liquid sulfur, what can we anticipate will happen?" Again too, the teacher needs to build explicit gestures into his nonverbal repertoire; when he verbally handles if–then relationships, he should supplement his words with distinct gestures that serve as nonverbal models.

MY OPINION In conveying opinions, body language is an important component of the message. A speaker often gestures toward himself, leans toward those who are listening, and emphasizes with his hands, arms, and head.

"This is my opinion" discussion groups can be organized for sharing opinions in which spontaneous body language will supplement words. Operating in five-person teams, each participant shares with teammates an opinion he has about a book, a movie, a TV show, a celebrity, a political figure, or a controversial issue. Youngsters join a team because of knowledge about and interest in the topic a team will be discussing. A sign-up sheet (see opposite page) can be posted on the coming events section of the bulletin board.

Youngsters sign for the topic of their choice, prepare their arguments either pro or con, and then meet in talk-teams at the designated time. Each group organizes itself so that first a pro speaker has the floor, then a con speaker. The moderator chairs the group.

SIGN UP HERE FOR OPINION SHARING TEAMS
THAT WILL MEET ON THURSDAY AT 2:30 P.M.

Team 1——Year-Round Daylight Savings Time

Moderator_____

Pro_____   _____

Con_____   _____

Team 2——Free Medical Care for All

Moderator_____

Pro_____   _____

Con_____   _____

Team 3——Jonathan Livingston Seagull

Moderator_____

Pro_____   _____

Con_____   _____

Team 4——Banning Cigarette Ads in Magazines

Moderator_____

Pro_____   _____

Con_____   _____

Team 5——All in the Family

Moderator_____

Pro_____   _____

Con_____   _____

Team 6——Watergate Affair

Moderator_____

Pro_____   _____

Con_____   _____

Team 7——The Mets

Moderator_____

Pro_____   _____

Con_____   _____

SIGHTLESS DISCUSSION   Schedule a sharing session in which pairs of youngsters talk about a topic of common interest, e.g., a movie or TV show that both youngsters have seen, an up-coming sports event, a project both are involved in, a hobby both enjoy, or a problem both share. But suggest that the youngsters sit back-to-back and *not* make eye contact; they must communicate only with words and voices. Youngsters follow up by writing a paragraph on how it feels to talk without receiving any visual feedback.

This activity can be carried out in the listening-speaking center. Pairs of youngsters can select a sightless discussion as an independent study activity, go to the center, discuss together, and write their reactions.

Next try a sightless discussion as an entire class activity. Youngsters should bring to class a large handkerchief to tie over their eyes. The discussion can be on any topic related to studies underway in the class. When children have talked for about ten minutes, they remove their blindfolds and react to such questions as:

- What clues did you miss during the sightless discussion?
- Did you feel a sense of dissatisfaction after you expressed an opinion and could get no reaction from facial expressions?
- Did you change your manner of expressing yourself when you realized that listeners could not see you?
- Did you change your posture or sitting position when you realized that others could not see you?
- Did you feel less conspicuous or ill-at-ease?

PUT ON YOUR OLD GREY BONNET!   Wearing a simple costume or manipulating simple props may get youngsters into the mood of a story they are reading and discussing and stimulate nonverbal expression of meanings. Some brief examples will clarify this statement:

- Children read and talk about cowboys in the Wild West. Donning cowboy hats may get them into the mood of the story and stimulate spontaneous role playing as a part of the discussion. Similar props to use in other contexts include baseball caps, football helmets, bandanas, wooly, warm snow hats, make-believe crowns, or sombreros.
- Children read and talk about a Halloween story. Wearing tall, pointed black hats made from rolled construction paper gets the youngsters into the story mood, and talk turns into role playing. Similarly, children can construct from paper firemen's hats, policemen's hats, sailors' hats, or conductors' hats to wear as they talk about stories.
- Young children talk about and plan for a cooking session in which they will make spaghetti sauce. Each young participant gets a discussion prop—a large spoon to gesture with during discussion. Other gesturing props to use on different occasions might be homemade magic wands, flags, and silk scarfs.
- Young children in kindergarten can make bunny ears that they tie on their heads as they listen to and talk about any one of Beatrix Potter's "The Story of Peter Rabbit" series. The wearing of flappy-floppy ears may stimulate head shaking and rabbit motions. Do the same with monster masks before talking about *Where the Wild Things Are,* with feathers and headbands before talking about an Indian story, and with long noses

before talking about *Pinocchio*. In each case little children can make their own props and then wear them as they listen to and talk about a story.

- Children can also become more intimately involved in stories they are hearing or reading by making the sound effects important in the stories. Keep available a supply of noise makers: whistles, bells, rattles, hammers, gongs, and rhythm band instruments. On a day in which youngsters encounter a noise-filled story, one child in the group can be in charge of producing sound effects to go with the story.

Teachers in Shrewsbury Borough, New Jersey, have carried the use of props one step further. Children climb aboard an old stagecoach when they read; the teachers don costumes to encourage the children to read. The result is heightened interest in reading as well as increased opportunity for non-verbal expression in story discussions.

CONTRIVED ACTIVITIES

POKER FACE   Children play lots of games in classrooms. There are the simple card games in which they draw word or sound cards and pair the cards as practice in grapheme and word recognition. There are the team games in which youngsters earn points for their group. In many such games, youngsters must hide their positive or negative feelings about the cards they have drawn or hold. In this situation the face, the voice, and the body should not reveal one's pleasure or displeasure.

Within game situations, children can play "Poker Face" simultaneously with the actual game they are playing. Youngsters can make poker faces and should try not to show through their voices how they feel. After a game sequence, children can talk about what gestures, tones, or expressions gave other children away.

NO PASSIVE PARTICIPANTS, PLEASE   An experimental discussion activity that has an element of fun is overt physical expression of positive and negative reactions to ongoing class discussion. The rules of the game are simple. As participants in a discussion comment, others show overtly through facial expressions, nodding and shaking their heads, hand gestures, and leaning motions of their bodies whether they agree or disagree.

Before playing the game, children talk about body language that shows agreement and disagreement, demonstrating facial expressions, gestures, and larger body motions as they talk. Then, during a discussion of a controversial issue, the rule is "No passive participants, please." Listeners must nonverbally react so that a speaker gets immediate feedback from listeners.

You can follow up with a talk time in which youngsters verbalize their feelings about getting such overt, immediate feedback and draw conclusions about the effect of listener feedback on a speaker. With older youths, follow-up talk can lead into discussion of why people often do not express their reactions so overtly and of why people sometimes hide their genuine feelings behind a masking smile.

CLAYBALLS   Nervous gesturing is common among

elementary school children. Youngsters twist, turn, tap feet and pencils, bite nails, suck fingers, rub hands back and forth across their desks, and roll paper. The motions, which Barbara Grant and Dorothy Hennings classified as self-adjusting motions in *The Teacher Moves: An Analysis of Non-verbal Activity* (Teachers College Press, 1971), are ways in which children release excess energy and tension.

To keep her third-grade children's hands occupied during large group discussions and to supply an energy outlet, Ms. Doris Morris has devised a system that works well for her. Each child is given a small ball of clay. During a discussion period, the youngsters roll the balls in their palms much in the manner that men in Greece manipulate worry beads. Amazingly, in her classroom, the itching, finger biting and sucking, foot jiggling, and twisting behavior characteristic of children of this age are less pronounced. You may want to experiment with Ms. Morris's approach to see if it works in your classroom.

TALKING IN A TOUCHING CIRCLE Students sit on the floor in a circle for discussion purposes; each student sits so that his or her arm touches the arm of the student next to him or her. Discussion travels around the touching circle. Later students talk about how touching affects communication.

TOUCH TO TALK As they sit around a table talking about a shared story or a controversial issue, older students can try a physical method for determining who will speak next. The person who wants to speak puts his or her hand out flat on the table. The person who has just commented touches the hand of the one who is to carry the conversation ball on; the person touched speaks and in turn touches the hand of the next participant.

A teacher of young children can use a similar technique to identify who will speak next in a small group situation. The teacher simply touches the extended hand of the child who is to answer, to do, to show, or to read.

With younger or older students, follow-up discussion, in which girls and boys express their reactions to the touching procedure, may elicit ideas about the messages that can be sent by physical contact.

THE CONVERSATION BALL   Another way of engineering a discussion situation in which there is less physical contact than in "Touch to Talk" is to use an actual conversation ball. The discussion starter holds a ball in his hand as he or she speaks; he or she then hands the ball to the participant who wants to speak next, who in turn speaks and then hands the ball on to another participant. This technique works well in situations in which youngsters are sitting on the floor together and would find extending their hands awkward. It also prevents numbers of children from talking at once or from calling out when they want to participate; the one who holds the ball has the floor.

After children have experimented with "Touch to Talk" and "The Conversation Ball," schedule a very short discussion in which youngsters talk about the advantages and the disadvantages of the two methods of controlling discussions, compare those methods to the traditional raising of hands, and suggest other methods for engineering conversations, which they later try out. Other techniques students may enjoy trying include passing the conversation ball by making eye contact, by leaning toward, by nodding, by smiling broadly, or by pointing toward the next participant.

SPEAKING WITH SILENCE Silence can be part of a message; silence can be used to emphasize a point, to gain attention, and to allow time for listeners to consider what has been said.

Youngsters can play with silence experimentally in class discussions. A student or teacher who has just made a discussion contribution that he or she really wants others to consider seriously raises his hand with thumb and finger making an O-shape. A general classroom operating rule is that no one participating in the discussion can say anything for ten seconds after the silence signal has been given so that everyone can think about the idea just expressed.

OBSERVER OF SILENCE During large group discussions, one student can be an observer of silence. He or she records when silent periods occur and what contribution the silence made to the discussion. At the end of the discussion, the silent participant shares his or her observations with the class.

A simple observation guide may be helpful for a first-time observer. Such a guide may include just two columns in which notes are recorded:

OBSERVING SILENCE	
WHEN SILENCE OCCURRED DURING DISCUSSIONS	**WHAT THE SILENCE SEEMED TO SAY**

OBSERVER OF GESTURES During general class discussion, a student can function as an observer of gestures. He is again a silent participant, this time watching for gestures used during the discussions. Using a guide, he records the gestures and the messages sent through gestures and reports on his observations at the end of the discussion period.

OBSERVING GESTURES	
IMPORTANT GESTURES USED DURING DISCUSSION	**WHAT THE GESTURES SEEMED TO SAY**

OBSERVER OF FACIAL EXPRESSIONS On another occasion, a silent discussion observer can focus on facial expressions. He watches for facial expressions used by participants to communicate ideas and feelings. Once again, he records his observations in tabular form and reports his observations at the end of the discussion.

OBSERVING FACIAL EXPRESSIONS	
FACIAL EXPRESSIONS OBSERVED DURING DISCUSSION	WHAT THE FACES SEEMED TO SAY

One caution! Students participating in a discussion should not know what behavior the observer is observing. Knowing that a certain type of behavior is being investigated by an observer, discussion participants may become self-conscious, feign facial expressions, or affect gestures. The same may be true of a teacher who knows that his or her gestures, uses of silence, or facial expressions are the focus of attention on a particular occasion.

Therefore, keep a grab bag of observational activities in the classroom. The bag is filled with slips on each of which is written an observational task such as:

- Observe and record uses of silence.
- Observe and record messages sent by facial expressions.
- Observe and record gestures used during class discussion.
- Observe and record words that were used and that really packed a punch.
- Observe and record any nonverbal signs that indicated participants were enjoying or not enjoying the discussion.
- Look for and record any features of the situation (ar-

rangement of furniture, placement of visual aids, position of students and teacher, ventilation, lighting, timing) that interfered with the discussion.

* Keep a record of the number of different students who participated verbally in the discussion.

Keep in readiness observational guides related to each of the tasks. After drawing a slip from the grab bag, a student who is to be the discussion observer goes to the file and selects the appropriate dittoed observational guide for recording what he sees. Only at the end of the discussion does the observer explain what he or she was looking for and what he or she discovered.

MOVING CHAIRS   At the beginning of a group talk session in which the teacher intends to take part, suggest that participants move their chairs closer together. When students have formed a tight group, ask them to guess what they are going to do. As children guess, respond with the question, "Why do you think that?" Children may answer that the way they were asked to sit gave them a clue about what they would be doing.

SAY IT WITH FEELING   A spoken word, phrase, or sentence not only communicates through the actual meanings of the word or words but through the way the word or words are spoken. To give youngsters opportunities to communicate through changes in tone, rate, loudness, pitch, and inflections, try the following activity.

Prepare a hand-out sheet comprised of two lists —a list of phrases describing the way in which words can be spoken and a list of words that can be spoken in a variety of ways:

IT'S HOW YOU SAY IT THAT IS IMPORTANT

I. WAYS OF SPEAKING A WORD OR SENTENCE:

WITH SADNESS	WITH DETERMINATION
WITH REGRET	WITH CONCERN
WITH FEAR	WITH LACK OF CONCERN
WITH HAPPINESS	WITH ENTHUSIASM
WITH PRIDE	WITH VENGEANCE
WITH DISGUST	WITH SURPRISE
WITH ANTICIPATION	WITH SARCASM

II. WORDS TO SPEAK:

PLEASE	OFTEN	WHEN	CRAZY
NEVER	SORRY	HOW	COME
GOOD	HELP	WHERE	NO
ME	OH	NEXT	YES
YOU	WHY	NOW	STOP

A child selects a word from part II of the hand-out sheet and speaks it with a feeling listed in part I. Other participants in the activity try to guess the feeling being expressed. The successful guesser becomes the next person to express a word with feeling.

Children can move from work with expressing single words to work with sentences. Again a hand-out sheet, such as the one on the opposite page, can serve as a discussion framework.

Children select a sentence from part II and express it in one of the ways suggested in part I. Once again, other youngsters guess the feeling being expressed.

To use this activity with younger children, you may have to simplify the feelings listed in part I and limit the number of feelings in part II to five or six,

SAY IT WITH FEELING

I. WAYS OF SPEAKING A SENTENCE:

AS IF YOU ARE EXPRESSING A POSSIBILITY
AS IF YOU ARE BREWING A CONSPIRACY
AS IF YOU ARE KIDDING AROUND
AS IF YOU ARE THREATENING
AS IF YOU ARE SURPRISED
AS IF YOU ARE TIRED
AS IF YOU ARE PLEADING
AS IF YOU ARE EXPLAINING
AS IF YOU ARE DISGUSTED
AS IF YOU ARE IN A HURRY
AS IF YOU COULD CARE LESS
AS IF YOU ARE AFRAID
AS IF YOU ARE UNHAPPY
AS IF YOU ARE STATING A FACT
AS IF YOU ARE FED UP
AS IF YOU ARE EXCITED
AS IF YOU ARE UNSURE
AS IF YOU CAN HARDLY WAIT

II. SENTENCES TO SPEAK:

THAT PROGRAM IS ON TONIGHT.!?
OH, I'LL DO THAT TOMORROW.!?
WILL YOU COME TOO.!?
THAT'S A NICE DRESS.!?
I LIKE SUZY.!?
I AM GOING HOME.!?
WELL, LET'S GET STARTED.!?
WHY DO YOU BOTHER.!?
I'LL SEE YOU LATER.!?
YOU BETTER NOT DO THAT.!?
I'LL BE RETURNING NEXT WEEK.!?
YOU TAKE CARE OF THE MONEY.!?
I'LL TAKE CARE OF THE SUPPLIES.!?
DO YOU UNDERSTAND WHAT YOU ARE DOING.!?
WHERE DID YOU PUT THE CANDY.!?
NOW, EVERYBODY, WE MUST WORK TOGETHER.!?

such as: speak as if you are—unhappy, scared, angry, happy, proud, excited. The teacher must prepare the hand-out sheets to meet the unique needs of his particular group of children.

With both older and younger children, the activity can be repeated. Later the youngsters can express meanings using a combination of vocal and physical effects; gestures, facial expressions, and vocal nuances can merge into a total message.

Try to conclude any of the sessions described in this activity with some generalizing about the ways people communicate. Youngsters can project such generalizations as:

* Sometimes we make our voices go up (or down) to show what we mean or how we feel.
* Sometimes we speak more slowly to get a feeling across.
* Sometimes we raise our voices to show how we feel.
* Sometimes we make a sentence into a question to express sarcasm, surprise, or doubt.

Conclusions can be recorded on charting paper and mounted on a bulletin board captioned How We Say What We Mean.

DESIGNING FOR TALKING The way furniture is arranged often communicates to participants in a situation what behavior is expected of them. To help students in upper grades gain understanding of the communicative potential of furnishings, involve students in an experiment dealing with different ways of physically organizing the room for small group discussion. Prepare a hand-out sheet (see opposite page) to kick off the experiment.

Distribute the hand-out. Students divide into four-person teams and select which way they will arrange themselves for group activity. Armed with charting paper and flow pens, they prepare seating designs and then discuss briefly the seating arrangement they chose and how it worked out in practice.

DESIGNING FOR TALKING

1. As we talk in discussion groups during the next two weeks, we are going to experiment with different ways of arranging chairs and desks and ways of sitting to determine what kind of mood is established by a specific arrangement and to determine the advantages of different arrangements.

2. Below are listed some ways of physically organizing talking sessions:
   A. Sit in a circle on the floor cross-legged. Leave very litle space between participants so that your arms almost touch.
   B. Arrange desks to form a square so that each group member can see the others.

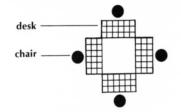

   C. Arrange desks so that the group leader is in center front and other group members face the leader.

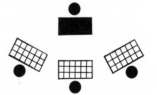

3. Today your task is, first, to select one of the seating arrangements listed above, then arrange yourselves in that pattern. Next sketch out on paper other arrangements for small group talk. Finally transfer your sketches to large charting paper and think about the advantages of each arrangement you designed.

At the end of the work session, youngsters share their findings with the total class. Group reporters explain the designs their groups have devised and drawn on charting paper; they compare possible advantages of each design. They also explain to the others their group reaction to the seating arrangement actually used that day.

The charts prepared can be mounted on the bulletin board. During the next two weeks, whenever a small group functions, members first select a seating arrangement from one of the posted charts and arrange themselves in that pattern. After they have completed their job, they take time to evaluate the seating arrangement, write a two- or three-sentence evaluation on an index card, and affix the card near the diagram showing that design.

At the end of the two-week period, students can draw conclusions about the effectiveness of different seating arrangements for group work and the kinds of messages each arrangement communicates to participants. The index cards posted on the bulletin board throughout the experimental period will serve as firsthand data on which to base conclusions.

MORE DESIGNS FOR TALKING Upper-elementary school youngsters may also investigate the messages communicated by the seating arrangements used for large group discussions. Employ a variety of seating arrangements for large group discussions during an experimental period; the arrangements may include:

- Students sitting on chairs arranged in parallel rows with the teacher or discussion leader standing in center-front.

- Students sitting on chairs in informal clusters with the teacher or leader standing in the front.
- Students sitting on chairs in a circle arrangement with the teacher or leader sitting as part of the circle.
- Students sitting randomly on the floor with the teacher or leader sitting on a hassock or on the floor.
- Students sitting on chairs in a square arrangement with the teacher or leader sitting at the front of the square.
- Students sitting in two facing lines with leader sitting somewhere in the line.

Variations may include having pencils and notebooks placed on desks before students begin to discuss, children being asked to carry pencils and notebooks with them to their spots on the floor, and children using a nod to indicate their desire to participate.

At the end of the experimental period, students can discuss in small groups their reactions to each arrangement the teacher used and the kinds of behavior they felt was required of them in each situation. Students can draw conclusions about what each design communicated by focusing on such questions as:

When the teacher stands up front, what does that tell you about his expectations for the session?

When the teacher has you discuss seated at your desks in rows, what does this tell you about his expectations?

When you sit on the floor for a discussion, does this change your attitude toward the discussion? Why? Why not?

When you are given pencils and notebooks at the beginning of the discussion period, what are you being told?

Does the place where the teacher positions himself communicate anything to you about what is expected?

Does sitting in a circle compared with sitting in a square affect communication?

Students can summarize conclusions on large charting paper for sharing with other groups.

SUMMARY THOUGHTS

Three thoughts have probably occurred to readers of this chapter. First, helping students acquire nonverbal communication skills important in discussion situations also helps students acquire verbal skills. In communicating, a speaker does not rely solely on verbal or nonverbal expression; nonverbal and verbal merge into the total message a speaker is sending. Therefore, a program to develop nonverbal skills must—by the nature of the beast—be part of a comprehensive language program that stresses self-expression.

Second, the subject content of discussions in which youngsters gesture, experiment with seating arrangements, or use props can be any of the subjects normally found in the curriculum—science, art, music, social science, mathematics, literature, or language. To teach communication skills, a teacher must by necessity involve youngsters in a variety of ideas and thought processes, so that they will have things to talk about. For this most basic of reasons—that students must talk about significant topics for discussions to have value—verbal-nonverbal discussion activities cannot be divorced from the rest of the curriculum.

Third, it is now probably obvious that verbal-nonverbal talk takes place in a variety of situations. People interact on a one-to-one basis, within small conversation groups, and in large discussion groups. Therefore, a teacher who wants to help students acquire both verbal and nonverbal communication skills must design many different discussion-conversation situations into the daily classroom program: student conversation pairs, small work teams, small talk groups, total class sharing sessions, reporting sessions, and teacher-student interactions. By building different types of talk into the ongoing curriculum, a teacher is providing opportunities for youth to try out nonverbal and verbal communication techniques in the kinds of situations encountered in everyday life.

VI: LET'S
JUST LISTEN

To be able to interpret the nonverbal expressions of others is just as important as being able to express oneself with more than words. The person who perceives more than the verbal messages sent to him has additional information on which to base his opinions and on which to take action. For instance, he may sense that an individual with whom he is talking is irritated, fearful, or hesitant and may handle the situation differently than he would if he based his actions solely on the verbal message received. Or he may sense that a person with whom he is talking is not attentive and may decide to wait for a more fortuitous moment to speak of important matters.

A program to develop nonverbal language skills, therefore, must have two emphases—one on expressing and one on interpreting. The activities in this chapter place children in the observer's role and ask them to interpret the nonverbal clues they are receiving. Some of the activities, such as picture reading, are rather easy. Others described near the end of the chapter are more sophisticated and require a higher level of analytical thinking. These probably are most appropriately used in the upper-elementary grades.

INTERPRETING PICTURES

WATCH THE EXPRESSION One of the easiest ways to start children interpreting nonverbal messages sent to them is through picture reading. Select large pictures in which facial expressions show how the person or persons feel about what is going on.

Some excellent picture series can be purchased that are especially good for encouraging interpretive activity. Developmental Learning Materials (3305 North Ashland Ave., Chicago, Illinois 60657) has two series: "The Many Faces of Childhood" and "The Many Faces of Youth." Each series is comprised of twelve, large black-and-white or color photographs in which such emotions as loneliness, pleasure, and fear are expressed. A teacher's guide suggesting ways of using the pictures accompanies each series. "The Many Faces of Childhood" can be appropriately used in K–3; "The Many Faces of Youth" is geared for upper grades, 4–8.

Another series, "Moods and Emotions" distributed by The Child's World, Inc. (Mankato, Minnesota) is comprised of slightly impressionistic colored drawings of children who are expressing through their faces and eyes the emotions they are feeling. Intended for use with primary-grade children, each picture focuses on a single emotion. One of the strengths of this material is that on the reverse side of each picture is a story centering on the emotion and suggested activity sequences in which children themselves can become physically involved in the feelings and can use their bodies to express feelings. A second picture series distributed by the same company, "The Many Moods of Mother Goose," has similar features but is probably useful only in kindergarten and first grade.

Franklin Watts' series "Man on the Move" can be used in much the same way but at the intermediate and upper-grade levels. The black-and-white photographs in the portfolio depict people interacting in emotionally explicit situations. Again the way the people in the picture feel can be read from their facial and bodily expressions as well as from situational clues.

These and similar picture materials clipped from magazines can be used in a discussion-type learning encounter in which youngsters talk about how the people in the pictures feel and express their feelings.

In addition, children can use the pictures as stimuli for written expression. Mount the pictures on a bulletin board, caption the board "Pick a Picture," and subcaption pictures with such questions as:

- What is this boy thinking?
- How does the girl in the picture feel?
- Would you want to be in this picture—why?
- What is going to happen next?

Individually children select a picture and react to its mood and feeling in written form; they may also select a picture as a small group activity, talk about how the picture makes them feel, and then act out those feelings nonverbally.

READ THE PICTURE   Don't forget the marvelously expressive faces found in picture books. For example, the faces of the creatures in Maurice Sendak's *Where the Wild Things Are* (Harper & Row, 1963) tell the story and can be "read"; Dr. Seuss' Horton in *Horton Hatches the Egg* (Random House, 1940) has determination, unhappiness, and pleasure written on his elephant face; and Samantha shows her grief physically in *Sam, Bangs and Moonshine* (Holt,

1966) by Evaline Ness when she realizes her moon-shine has nearly caused disaster for her playmate and her cat. All of these expressions can be inter-preted as part of the story. Other titles especially good for this purpose are: Charlotte Zolotow's *The Hating Book* (Harper & Row, 1969) and *The New Friend* (Abelard-Schuman, 1968), and Ellen Raskin's *Nothing Ever Happens on My Block* (Atheneum, 1966).

Then there are the wordless books that are gain-ing in popularity. Children interpret mood and ac-tion from the picture sequences, facial expressions, and changes in the physical position of people and things in the drawings. Have children "read":

Mayer, Mercer. *A Boy, A Dog and A Frog* (Dial, 1967). A boy and a dog venture out to catch a frog.

Mayer, Mercer. *A Boy, A Dog, A Frog and a Friend* (Dial, 1971). A large turtle plays tricks on a boy, a dog, and a frog.

Meyer, Renate. *Vicki*. (Atheneum, 1969). A little girl ex-periences loneliness and friendlessness.

Goodall, John. *Shrewbettina's Birthday*. (Harcourt, Brace, 1971). Shrewbettina progresses from being robbed to having a party all in one day.

Hamberger, John. *A Sleepless Day* (Four Winds Press, 1973). An owl spends a frustrating day trying to find a safe, quiet, dry place to sleep.

Hamberger, John. *The Lazy Dog* (Four Winds Press, 1971). A large shaggy dog chases a runaway ball and returns home exhausted just as his master wakes up and is ready to play.

As they "read," ask the children how they know how the characters are feeling and what is happening. In most of these books, clear detail makes interpretation an enjoyable experience.

SILENT MOVIES   Show a regular sound movie, but switch off the sound track. Children interpret what is going on in the film simply from the action and from background clues. After viewing the "silent" movie, children divide into groups; each group writes a brief outline of the action, suggesting what was occurring in the film. Each group reads its outline to the class. Then the sound is switched on, and the film is viewed again to determine which group came closest to the actual spoken story line. Members of that group can explain which nonverbal clues were most significant in their interpretation.

WRITE THE SCRIPT   A similar activity can be carried out using story filmstrips that are wordless. Educational Enrichment Materials (83 East Avenue, Norwalk, Connecticut 06851) distributes silent filmstrips of such wordless books as Martha Alexander's *Out! Out! Out!* (Dial, 1968) and *Bobo's Dream* (Dial, 1970) and Mercer Mayer's *Frog, Where Are You?* (Dial, 1969). Children view a strip, interpret action and facial expressions, and write the story that goes with the strip.

Sound filmstrips of stories can be used in much the same way, but without the sound. See if children can "read" the story using only the pictorial clues. Only after youngsters have written their own story line to accompany the strip should they listen to the sound track. Sources of sound filmstrips include Scholastic Magazines, Inc., Teaching Resources Inc., Weston Woods, and Miller-Brody Productions.

COMIC PUZZLE Black out with felt pen the balloons of a comic strip. *Blondie, Nancy,* and *Peanuts* are particularly good for this purpose. Children can interpret the mood and action and write what they think the characters are saying.

Figuring out such comic strip language can be followed up with the creation of original comic strips. Children select a mood word (lonely, mean, furious, excited, bored, frantic, downcast, rejected, humble) and build comic strips around the feeling communicated by the word. In carrying out the activity, children will inevitably draw actions and facial expressions to express feelings.

To make the latter activity easier for children to handle, cut 9 x 12 inch manila construction paper into 4½ x 12 inch strips. Children divide the 12 inch length into four 3 inch blocks. Each block represents one episode in the story line, which can be told totally through nonverbal devices or through a combination of verbal and nonverbal expressions. For longer stories, children can tape strips together so that more blocks are available for story writing.

When numbers of children have created a comic, staple all the "bored" comics to a large piece of brown paper, funny paper-style, and title them The Bored Comics. Staple "mad" comics to another sheet and title them The Mad Comics. The same can be done with The Mean Comics, The Downcast Comics, The Silly Comics, and so on. Upper-grade children can take their funny papers down to the first and second grades to share with the younger children.

READING BODY TALK

HOW DO YOU FEEL TODAY? Mount a good-sized mirror over a sink or over a counter where children tend to stand. Next to the mirror mount a chart that asks:

```
HOW DO YOU FEEL TODAY?
LOOK AND SEE

HAPPY?
SAD?
TIRED?
ANGRY?
GLAD TO BE HERE?
CURIOUS?
LONELY?
```

FACES Use the book *Faces* by Barbara Brenner with photographs by George Ancona (E. P. Dutton, 1970) to start children reading messages sent through changing facial expressions. In *Faces* readers see close-ups of lips, a nose, an ear, a mouth, eyes, and a smile; they get a feel for what it is like to speak to a friend face-to-face. Use the book to motivate discussion of the different kinds of smiles people can smile, the different ways we can hold our mouths, and the expressions we can put on our faces to cover up how we really feel. When children begin to tell about a kind of smile or a way of using the eyes to send messages, encourage them to show rather than to tell; suggest, "Show us what you mean, Johnnie."

READ THE MESSAGE "Read the message" is a team game that can follow up discussion about the meaning of facial expressions. The class is divided into two teams. One youngster momentarily leaves the room, while a member of his team draws an emotion slip from a grab bag. In the bag are slips of paper bearing a range of feeling words—resentment, irritation, exhaustion, boredom, attentiveness, loneliness, pleasure, fear, hopelessness and the like. When the youngster returns, his teammates make facial expressions that communicate the feeling they have drawn from the grab bag.

This is a facial-expressions-only game, so no physical activity is allowed. The guesser has only one or two minutes to guess. If he is successful, his team earns a point; if he is unsuccessful, the emotion slip is returned to the bag, and the next team takes a turn.

HOW WE KNOW Involve young children in a brief discussion of how we can tell when someone is happy. Begin with the question, "What do we mean when we say, 'You look happy today.'?" As children describe the way happy people look and act, encourage them to show by putting on appropriate facial expressions and by making appropriate gestures.

Children can follow through with an art activity in which they paint a picture depicting happy people or draw faces on paper bag puppets that express happy feelings. Fingerpaint is an excellent medium for showing happy faces.

The same activity can be carried out with other feelings—mean, lonesome, tired, sad, and so forth. Actually, discussion can involve youngsters with all

these feelings, and they can select the feeling they
want to paint. Then, too, related written activities
can be an option for children who are investigating
body language; in poetry or prose, they can express:

• How they feel and look when they are sad (happy,
  lonely, mean, tired, scared).
• What makes them feel sad (happy, lonely, mean, tired,
  scared).

HOW DO WE FEEL?   At the end of a day, as a
class activity in the lower grades, help children compile a "Feeling Chart":

FEELING	WHO FEELS THIS WAY	HOW WE KNOW HE FEELS THIS WAY
TIRED		
CHEERFUL		
UNHAPPY		
ANGRY		
CONSIDERATE		
EXCITED		

Next to the feeling words, the children can list the
names of boys, girls, the teacher, or special teachers
who showed these feelings during the day. Then
the children suggest how they knew that these individuals felt that way. Ask such questions as: "Did
he talk happy? Did he sound happy? Did he walk
happy? Did his face read happy? What happy-
appearing things did he do?" to encourage in-depth

perception. Guard against children making unkind comments that could hurt other children's feelings.

WATCH FOR FEELING CLUES   Older youngsters can use feeling charts as individual observation guides; in this case an observer fills in the feeling he observes another showing on a particular occasion, the person or persons observed, when the observation occurred, and how he knew how the observed person was feeling. With children in upper-elementary grades use the words inference and data to describe the observer's judgment about another person's feelings and about the actual observations.

WHAT FEELING? (INFERENCE)	WHO?	WHEN?	HOW I KNEW HE FELT THIS WAY (DATA OF OBSERVATION)

Feeling charts can be made as an individual activity carried on during field trips or as an ongoing assignment for children to complete wherever they encounter other people—in supermarkets, on the streets, in the playground, during all school activities, at home, on a fire drill line, at a sports event, and the like.

BE THE SILENT OBSERVER   Upper-grade children can compile even more complex observation guides on which they can record nonverbal data about people. After they have been involved in nonverbal observations for several weeks, ask them to study the data on which they have based their inferences. They will probably cite such data as: he spoke sharply, he slumped his shoulders, he had a spark in his eye, he tapped his foot, or his shoulders shook. Have the children try to organize these specific kinds of observations into broad categories by asking questions:

- How can we group all these nonverbal data into groups that have something in common?
- Which ones deal with the way words were spoken?
- Which ones deal with facial expressions?

Through classification activities students can develop categories to guide future observations and can compile an Interpretation Guide.

TECHNICAL INTERPRETATION GUIDE

NAME OF OBSERVER_____

OCCASION OF OBSERVATION_____

TONE OF VOICE_____

VOLUME OF VOICE_____

RATE OF SPEAKING_____

PITCH OF VOICE_____

GESTURES USED_____

FACIAL EXPRESSIONS_____

STANCE OR POSTURE_____

OVERALL BODY MOTIONS_____

DRESS_____

MANNERISMS THAT TEND TO BE REPEATED_____

(AND/OR ANY OTHER CATEGORIES CHILDREN SUGGEST)

An Interpretation Guide can be used to analyze numerous situations:

* A workman going about his task.
* Several people conversing.
* A shopper in a supermarket.
* Someone listening to the teacher.
* A person waiting on line.
* Several youngsters playing together.

The data recorded on the guide are the basis for inferring how the observed person felt about a situation.

WHAT WE LIKE AND DISLIKE What people like or dislike often is communicated nonverbally by the amount of time they spend on an activity or with another person, by the distance they maintain between themselves and another person or thing, by the way they look at things around them, by the way they touch things, or by the way they hold their bodies. To help children think about the ways people get to know about other people's likes and dislikes, make a large bulletin board on which all the children's names are listed:

HOW WE LEARN ABOUT PEOPLE				
HERE WE ARE	OUR LIKES	CLUES TO OUR LIKES	OUR DISLIKES	CLUES TO OUR DISLIKES
BRUCE				
CAROLYN				
DENISE				
TEACHER'S NAME				

At the end of a day, children take turns suggesting things that other children in the class as well as the teacher like and dislike, and indicate *how they know*. To start the activity going, the teacher can use himself as a model: "What do I like? dislike? How do you know?" Spend only a short time each day with the activity, but try to add to the chart each day. Suggest that children check their inferences made on previous days to see if the inferences made are really valid.

As items are added to the chart, it may be possible to draw conclusions of a general nature; children can conclude simply that gestures, body stance, distance, use of time, physical contact, and facial expressions are all clues to a person's likes and dislikes.

This activity can be extended to individual observations carried out by older youngsters. A boy or girl can list the names of people he or she encounters everyday: the principal, the next door neighbor, members of his or her family, the school crossing guard, or the school nurse. He or she records what these people appear to like and dislike and on what data he or she has based that opinion. An individual observation guide can be structured as:

OBSERVATION GUIDE				
PERSON	WHAT HE LIKES	OBSERVATIONAL DATA	WHAT HE DISLIKES	OBSERVATIONAL DATA

DESCRIBING   Children in small groups select a favorite TV personality and watch that person for several weeks using the Interpretation Guide as a framework for their observations. At the end of the assigned period of observation, youngsters work in their groups to write a descriptive paragraph about their TV celebrity that includes both verbal and non-verbal characteristics: words he tends to repeat; characteristic gestures; tone, pitch, and loudness of voice; mannerisms; stance; use of eyes and facial expressions; dress; overall appearance; and speed of activity. The description does NOT include the individual's name, the name of the program, or the kind of performer he is.

Each group prepares a preliminary draft and then prints a final description on large sized paper to mount on a bulletin board captioned "Guess the Star." Under each description, the groups mount a small box with a slit in the top. Other children try to guess who the star is, write their guesses on slips of paper, and drop them in the appropriate boxes. After children have had sufficient time to guess and also to build up suspense as to whether they were right, open the boxes. Each team names its celebrity and the number of correct guesses.

The same activity can be carried on using other categories of people. For instance, children in small groups can select one of the teachers in the school, a political figure, or a sports personality to observe for a period of time. Again the group builds a description based on the person's characteristic ways of expressing himself. The description is mounted on the bulletin board, and other students guess.

Note: This activity provides an added bonus of correlating consideration of nonverbal communication with written expression; here students are engaged in purposeful writing for other children will read their written words.

INTERPRETING IMPRESSIONS Sometimes people who want to create a particular impression use nonverbal messages to build an effect. Children can begin to understand how certain gestures can create an impression by an activity that combines pantomime with systematic analysis.

Ask for volunteers to pantomime the following:

Create the impression that you are really interested in what a platform speaker is saying.

Create the impression that you are completely bored by what is going on around you.

Create the impression that you are completely engrossed in an individual project on which you are working and do not want to be disturbed.

Create the impression that you are very relaxed and enjoying a social gathering.

Create the impression that you are confident.

Create the impression that you are shy and afraid.

After several children have tried each impression, divide youngsters into six groups. Give each group a felt marker and a big piece of charting paper; each group is assigned one of the impressions just pantomimed. Groups list on their charts the kinds of gestures, motions, poses, or facial expressions people tend to interpret as interest, boredom, engrossed preoccupation, relaxation, confidence, and shyness.

NOT JUST ONE MEANING A specific gesture or facial expression may not have a single meaning in every situation in which it is used. For example, touching someone on the shoulder may mean any number of things—stop doing that, I care about you, I sympathize with you, that's all right, be quiet, or wait a moment. To know which meaning to assign to a nonverbal act, one must interpret the act within the context that it occurs. To help children develop skill in hypothesizing possible meanings that a nonverbal expression can convey, try a group activity.

The class can divide into three-person teams. Each team works with a piece of experience chart paper on which is listed a nonverbal expression. Each group brainstorms, identifying the many meanings the nonverbal expression can convey and listing them on the paper.

Nonverbal expressions that are workable include:

Someone smiles.
Someone moves closer to you.
Someone next to whom you
 are sitting moves farther away.
Someone grabs your hand.
Someone points at you.
Someone waves at you.
Someone pounds the table.
Someone holds his hand up,
 palm outward toward you.
Someone shakes his head.
Someone puts his hand to his eyes.
Someone points toward the door.

After the teams have finished their task, schedule a reporting session in which each team shares its findings. The charts developed during the work session can be posted around the room and used as a basis for discussion of the overall question, "What determines which meaning an observer assigns to a nonverbal expression?" A way to get the discussion rolling is to focus on specific interpretations of an expression:

- When might a person interpret a smile as a sign of approval? as a sign of general enjoyment? as a mask to cover up real feelings? as a mask to cover up preoccupation with something else?
- Under what conditions might a person be correct in interpreting a hand raised to head as a sign of a headache? of tiredness? of a mannerism? of boredom? of concentrated thought?

Working from questions such as these, youngsters can conclude that:

- Gestures and facial expressions have many different meanings.
- Sometimes the meanings depend as much upon the receiver as upon the sender.
- Meanings must be interpreted in terms of the situation in which the expressions occur.
- Sometimes a gesture or facial expression can carry a meaning almost opposite to the meaning commonly assigned, e.g., a smile can mean "I told you so!" which is not the friendly meaning generally associated with a smile.
- Sometimes a facial expression or gesture can be used to cover up what one is really feeling.

MORE THAN ONE MEANING   Youngsters who have worked through the simple gestures and facial expressions listed in the preceding activity can go on to brainstorm the meanings that more complex nonverbal actions can communicate. Working again in three-person teams and recording their findings on charting paper with felt pen, older elementary-school youngsters can identify the many meanings of the following nonverbal expressions:

A person you know passes you in the school hall without making any signs of recognition.

A person walks particularly straight—shoulders thrown back and head held high.

A person with whom you are talking keeps looking out the window rather than looking at you.

A person keeps scratching his leg.

A girl keeps fiddling with a dangling necklace as you talk to her.

A person keeps you waiting for an appointment for more than an hour.

A person selects the comfortable chair and leaves the hard straight chair for you.

A person is running down the street.

A person always keeps his books piled in neat stacks on his desk.

A person sits tapping his fingernails on the desk.

A young boy is always dressed in dirty blue jeans and T-shirt.

A person stares at you.

A person walks up very close to you.

Again the question the teams are handling is "What messages do these nonverbal actions send to you?" Since in the preceding activity students have come to some understanding that the situation in which an action occurs gives a clue to its actual meaning, team members can go on to consider other questions: "Under what conditions would a particular action carry a specific meaning? How do we decide the meaning to assign?"

Group sharing of findings is the next step. Once more, the sharing period is a good time for formulating conclusions about the ways people may use nonverbal language to mask genuine feelings and to create specific impressions. It is a time for formulating conclusions about the messages people send just by the way they look at someone, by the way they dress, by the way they walk, or by the way they handle time and distance. It is a time for considering mannerisms, actions people repeat without consciously realizing what they are doing, and what mannerisms tell us about an individual. Discussion of mannerisms can lead to students' identifying their own mannerisms and considering ways of overcoming mannerisms that prove annoying to others and that block communication.

READING NONVERBAL DIRECTIONS In this activity the teacher gives directions without using words. Children must follow the directions to complete the task; they must watch actions closely or they will not know what to do. Some suggested directions to give nonverbally are:

- Give assignments for a reading or writing activity:
  1. Hold up a specific book containing assignment material.
  2. Open to the required spot in the book and hold up the page.

3. Take out and hold up the writing tool or kind of paper to be used.
4. Hold paper up against board, writing name, date, and title in appropriate spot.
5. Point to specific sections of book to be read; make reading gestures to show that it is to be read.
6. Point to specific questions to be answered.
7. Walk to container where students are to deposit finished papers; drop paper in to show youngster what to do when the assignment is completed.

- Demonstrate a paper cutting or folding activity. Show how to cut paper in half and fold into squares to make comic strips.
- Demonstrate a sports or dance activity.
- Demonstrate how to measure or rule off a paper into squares or blocks to prepare spaces for mathematics problems.
- Demonstrate how to do a technical task such as: how to handle a phonograph record, how to light a Bunsen burner, how to set up a ringstand for holding and heating a flask, how to insert a piece of glass into a one-hole rubber stopper, how to bend glass, how to thread a filmstrip projector, how to operate a cassette tape recorder. (In each of these examples, observing students write down the sequence of steps in the process being demonstrated nonverbally and then try it themselves.)
- Show young children how to walk on tiptoe from one area of the room to another, how to tie shoes, how to form letters in manuscript, or how to carry chairs into the storytelling area.

Interpreting such nonverbal messages as these can be a part of the daily "listening" activity of the class.

IGNORE THE ACTION   Simon Says is a direction-giving game that illustrates to children the impact of nonverbal messages. All players stand up. A leader stands facing the class. He shouts out directions for nonverbal actions players must perform. Simultaneously he performs actions that may or may not conform with his spoken directions. Typically given directions include:

Simon Says—thumbs up, thumbs down, touch your toes, arms over head, touch right ear, touch left ear, wiggle your nose, shake your head, nod your head, hold your palms up, hold your palms down, touch right eye, touch left eye. . .

If the action is fast, sooner or later a player does what the leader does, not what the leader says to do. That player is out. The last player to remain is the new leader.

A table variety of Simon Says is the game Peter Pay. Players sit around a table with one player as leader. He calls out three kinds of commands in rapid fire order. The first is "Peter Pay." At that command, players must extend the index finger of both their hands and alternately strike the fingers rapidly on the edge of the table. The second command is "Buck." At that command, players stand both their hands on the table using thumb and fingers as props. At the third command, "Platt" players place both hands palms downward, flat on the table. To trick the players, the leader calls out a command but puts his hands in one of the two other positions. If commands are given in rapid fire succession, players will sooner or later do what the leader does, not what he commands to be done.

After playing the game on several occasions, youngsters can talk about why they fell into the nonverbal trap. Such a discussion may reinforce in youngsters' minds the growing understanding that actions sometimes speak louder than words.

WATCH THE TEACHER "SPEAK" Body language often communicates basic substantive meanings; for instance, a person raises his hand with palm held outward to communicate "Stop!" Such body language is frequently seen in classrooms as youngsters raise their hands to indicate interest in participating and as a teacher uses gestures to give directions.

To help children become more explicitly aware of classroom body language, prepare a chart similar to the following on large paper and mount it on a bulletin board. Use the chart as a basis for classroom discussion of body language. The specific messages in the left column should be those nonverbal motions the teacher knows he or she tends to repeat in classroom interaction.

Ask youngsters to tell what meanings they associate with each of the motions listed in the left column. As youngsters propose meanings, a student scribe records a brief description in the middle column. Children also suggest the conditions when that motion takes on the specific meaning, e.g., in a discussion when the teacher points at a student, it means he is to speak. Since there is more than one way to send any of these messages, children should give as many different meanings for a motion as they can think of.

THE TEACHER SPEAKS		
MOTIONS	MEANINGS	CONDITIONS
POINTS		
WALKS TOWARD STUDENT		
NODS HEAD		
CLAPS HAND		
SCRATCHES HEAD		

Leave plenty of space at the bottom of the left column for additional nonverbal motions that the children observe the teacher using. Ask children to be particularly observant of the teacher's way of sending messages nonverbally and to keep notes during successive days. At the end of a day schedule a brief session in which children can add to the chart further actions observed during the day.

When a substantial chart of motions and meanings has been compiled, involve youngsters in generalizing about how body language is used. One conclusion that can be drawn is that a particular gesture, e.g., pointing, has different meanings depending on the situation in which it is used.

WATCH THE STUDENTS "SPEAK" A related activity focuses students' attention on the motions they use in the classroom to communicate meanings to the teacher and to one another. Working in observation-recording groups, youngsters can develop charts captioned The Students Speak; the chart again can be designed with three columns: motions, meanings, conditions. To start the ball rolling, the teacher may suggest one obvious student motion—raising the hand. After that, the groups list all the motions they know they use in classroom interactions. Schedule a class generalizing session after the groups have worked out their charts by filling in the columns; use the session for comparing group charts and drawing conclusions.

WE'RE ON TV   If your school is fortunate enough to own video-taping equipment, it has a role to play in the study of body language. You can simply set up the camera focusing it on the entire class. While replaying the tape, the class can identify substantive meanings sent physically during the session and complete the charts suggested in the activities called Watch the Teacher "Speak" and Watch the Students "Speak." An individual child can privately replay the tape in the listening corner of the room to identify the kinds of meanings he or she tends to communicate nonverbally.

THEY'RE ON TV   Groups of children can undertake an interpretive project using video-taping equipment owned by a school. They tape action in progress—in the assembly hall, in the hallways, in the cafeteria, or on the playground. If the school faces on a street, they can tape sounds and actions outside the window. If granted permission, they can tape meetings of the school board, town council, or other groups where interaction—both verbal and nonverbal—is fast and sometimes emotional. The tapes can serve as data for studying nonverbal clues.

WAYS OF SAYING IT WITHOUT WORDS At the beginning of the week, a bulletin board caption can announce: Twenty-five Ways To Say "That's Good!" Without Words. Tie a felt-tipped pen to the board and mount a box of cardboard strips at the bottom of the board. During independent study or seat work periods, a child can print on a strip a way to say "good" without using words and mount the strip on the board. At the end of the week, the class can discuss the board, suggesting the conditions under which the actions listed actually do mean good and the conditions under which the actions could have a different meaning.

Bulletin board captions for future weeks can include: Twenty-five Ways To Say "I Like You" Without Opening My Mouth! . . ., To Say "Yes" Wordlessly . . ., To Say "No" Without Using Words, or . . ., To Say "I Don't Like That" Without Opening My Mouth!

INTERPRETING LITERARY DESCRIPTIONS Read to children short passages from prose and poetry that describe a person in terms of his actions and expressions. For instance, read the description of Robert Browning's "The Pied Piper of Hamelin":

> Into the street the Piper stept
>   Smiling first a little smile,
> As if he knew what magic slept
>   In his quiet pipe the while;
> Then, like a musical adept,
> To blow the pipe his lips he wrinkled,
> And green and blue his sharp eyes twinkled,
> Like a candle-flame where salt is sprinkled;

Ask the children: "If you saw such a man, what impression would you get? What nonverbal clues give you this impression?"

Charles Dickens has written some great passages of description that can be used in a similar way; Rudyard Kipling, Longfellow, and Robert Louis Stevenson are additional sources of descriptive material that build concrete pictures of the way characters act and look.

If you want to correlate nonverbal study with written expression, follow-up with youngsters' writing and drawing descriptions of real, imaginary, or story book characters they have encountered.

TV COMMERCIALS Assign nonverbal interpretation of TV commercials as an optional out-of-class activity. Youngsters can watch El Exigente, The Demanding One, commercials to identify the nonverbal ways he "says" he is the demanding one. Students can list or draw the ways he "says" this. In class, youngsters can role play the demanding one and affect the gestures, stance, and facial expressions of El Exigente; other youngsters can role play the waiting coffee-growers whose economy depends on the demanding one's liking their cup of coffee. Youngsters can go on to role play a skit in which the demanding one gets a cup of coffee he rejects or a skit in which the demanding one becomes an undemanding one.

Use such a session to motivate continued analytical interpretation of TV commercials. Each youngster can select a commercial and try to identify the nonverbal devices the TV commercial producer is using to put his message across—facial expressions, props, gestures, sound effects, and action. The observation period can extend for as long as two weeks as children wait to look at several reruns of the commercial they have selected. Each youngster lists the nonverbal devices on a 5 by 7 index card. The cards can be posted on a bulletin board entitled "What's the TV Message?" and can be used as motivation for further discussion of such devices as props, sound effects, and use of distance and timing as part of a message. An activity such as this can make children more aware of the nonverbal devices that commercials use to persuade viewers to go out and buy products they may not need or want.

WATCH THE BODY SPEAK   An optional out-of-class assignment for older students who have had considerable experience interpreting nonverbal clues is to watch the bodies of performers on TV talk shows and to note the messages they send nonverbally. A series of questions can serve as a guide for observing and interpreting:

- How does Mr. X hold his body? Does he sit in a relaxed manner? How does he position his legs? his arms? In what position does he hold his head? Is there one position that he tends to assume most often or that seems characteristic of him?
- What gestures does he tend to repeat? Is there a particular facial expression that characterizes him?
- How physically active is he? Is he always moving around in his seat? gesturing? moving his head as he talks? changing his position? changing his facial expression? looking around? Or is he relatively still, physically

using only limited motion to express meanings? Does he rely almost entirely on verbal expression?

* What mannerisms does he exhibit? Are there nonverbal actions that he repeats so that the actions become obviously annoying to the listener?
* Does he seem to want to get closer to others with whom he is communicating? Does he lean toward them? Does he touch someone on the arm?
* How is he dressed?
* Are there any nonverbal clues that give away the performer's underlying nervousness? Are there nonverbal clues that suggest that the performer on the talk show is trying to communicate messages not representative of his true feelings? that he is trying to cover up his true feelings and thoughts?

Children who have pursued this activity individually can gather together in small discussion groups to share their observations, and perhaps, to formulate conclusions about the kind of person the TV performer really is and the kinds of meanings that can be read from specific nonverbal acts. After participating in their own talk session, children may apply the questions to their own nonverbal behavior during the session and try to perceive the messages they sent nonverbally. If video-taping equipment is available, the taping camera can record the session, and individual children can later study their own nonverbal messages as they watch the replay in the private classroom listening corner.

RED HOT   In any culture, colors have certain meanings associated with them, and a person may interpret a particular situation in terms of those cultural meanings. Children can begin to analyze the meanings associated with colors through books that deal directly with color-word relationships. Read to primary school youngsters such books as:

Robert Wolff's *Seeing Red* (Scribners, 1968). Explores some of the meanings sent by red.
Robert Wolff's *Feeling Blue* (Scribners, 1968). Treats some of the meanings of blue and how those meanings have been translated into expressions such as "feeling blue," "bluenoses," and "bluestockings."
Robert Wolff's *Hello Yellow!* (Scribners, 1968). Handles such meanings of yellow as coward and happy.
Janet Wolff's *Let's Imagine Colors* (Dutton, 1963). Gives literal meanings of color, encourages children to think about objects associated with specific colors, and can be used to help children explore some figurative meanings associated with colors.

As a follow up, children can write and illustrate their own color books in which they express meanings associated with colors; they can call their books by figurative titles like "Red Hot!"

THINKING ABOUT NONVERBAL MEANINGS An upper-grade class is divided into five-person discussion teams. Give each group a mimeographed sheet of the following situational descriptions. Groups talk about and list possible messages they might receive in each situation; they describe to one another similar situations in which they have been an actual participant or observer.

Problem Situations For Team Discussion
1. Your friend is supposed to come to play with you at

2:30 p.m. He comes at four o'clock and says he is late because he was playing ball with the kids on the street. What message does his being late send to you?

2. Two people are talking in the corner of a room. When you enter, they move closer together, begin to whisper, and turn their backs to you. What message do you receive nonverbally?

3. A teacher darts into the classroom, hastily picks up the papers scattered around the room, straightens things that are out of place, grabs up a stack of papers, and glances at his or her watch. You are watching through the window. What message do his or her actions send to you?

4. You see two people walking down the street; they are holding hands, looking intently at one another as they talk, and walking very close to one another. What messages do their actions send to you, the observer?

5. You are talking with a friend. As you talk to him, he keeps glancing at his wrist watch. What message might you receive from his actions?

6. You see a boy who has on a shabby jacket, a shoe with a loose sole, no socks, and a pair of patched pants that are dirty. What impression do you get from his clothes?

7. You see a fellow who has on a jacket of the latest fashion, a real sharp tie, and trousers that flair just right. Every hair on his head is in place, shoes are polished, and his striped shirt hasn't a wrinkle. What impression do you get from his clothes?

8. You see a mother holding a child by the hand in the supermarket. The mother keeps jerking the child's hand. When the child stumbles, the mother pulls the

child along. When the child cries out, the mother slaps the child on the hand. What message do you get from the mother's actions?

9. You are called to the principal's office. When he sees you coming, he smiles and waves for you to come in. He pulls a chair up next to his desk and gestures toward it, indicating that he wants you to sit there. What message do you get without words? Do you think you are in trouble?

10. You get called to the principal's office. The school secretary takes you in and stands you in front of the principal's desk. The principal looks up from his papers and stares at you without speaking. He doesn't ask you to sit down. What message do you get? Could you be in trouble?

After group discussion, teams select reporters to share their findings with the entire class. Reporters sit on stools, desks, or boxes arranged in a semicircle at the front of the room and summarize the thinking of their group on each problem situation.

When the reporters have considered each problem situation and class members have made additional comments, students return to their groups armed with felt-tipped pens, large experience story paper, and a question to be answered, "What kinds of nonverbal actions give us clues about how a person feels or what a person is thinking?" Groups develop a list of such clues and print the list on the paper for later mounting. Suggest that the groups give their lists a general title, so that readers will know what it is a list of.

Note 1: The problem situations included in this activity deal primarily with people's use of time, distance, other people, and objects in their environment. From the lists drawn up by the groups, children can draw conclusions about the communicative value of these environmental features.

Note 2: Again, if the school owns videotaping equipment, cameras can be focused on the entire class as it is involved in team discussions. Later in the privacy of the listening station, individuals can view the tape and study their own nonverbal clues.

THROUGH ROSE-COLORED GLASSES An episode in the *All in the Family* television series forcefully makes the point that what an individual perceives in a situation is often more dependent on his own values, interests, and prejudices than on what actually happens. In the episode, the audience first sees how the very conservative Archie Bunker views a particular happening, then sees how his very liberal son-in-law Mike views the identical happening, and finally sees what "really" has happened. In this situation—as in real life situations—each person's perceptions are influenced by the rose-colored glasses through which he views the world.

To help youngsters realize that the messages they receive are very much dependent on their own hangups, stage an emotion-charged incident. Plan ahead with two youngsters who will pretend to have a fight that you do not see; your back is turned. All the other students must write down what happened so you can find out what occurred. Of course, no two stories will be exactly the same, and that fact can be the basis for a discussion of factors that determine how a person perceives a situation.

Be on the alert for actual emotional incidents that youngsters can describe. Ask several students to give their interpretations of what happened. Again, each on-looker can be encouraged to think about why he perceived' the incident as he did and to share his thoughts in a general discussion.

Older students can undertake complex analyses of the "glasses" through which they view the world. Each student can compile his own list of:

> Things I like to do.
> Things I dislike doing.
> Colors I prefer.
> Things I think are important.
> Things I think are unimportant.
> Ways of talking that bother me.
> Music I dislike.
> Hair styles I like.
> Hair styles I detest.
> Clothing styles I can't stand.
> Etc.

At times when youngsters need to draw conclusions about things going on around them, they can refer back to their self-analyses to see if they can figure out which of their unique likes and dislikes made them perceive an event the way they did.

SUMMARY THOUGHTS

You can incorporate activities similar to the ones described in this chapter into the context of most ongoing classroom work. For example, in a reading experience—even with a basal reader—youngsters can interpret feelings and ideas from the pictures and from passages of description about the way a character looked, the way he smiled, or the way he walked. Look for places in a story to ask, "How do you think Mr. James looked (walked, acted, held his shoulders) when that happened?" or "What expression do you think Martha had on her face when she heard that she had won?"

On field trips look for nonverbal actions to interpret. Returning to the bus, you might ask: "Do you think our guide was happy with us?" "What kind of a person was our guide?" "Do you think he/she enjoys his/her work?" Back in the classroom, ask the same type of questions about the bus driver, encouraging children to identify the nonverbal behavior on which they based their opinions.

Interpretation of nonverbal expressions can also be part of regular class discussion. Ask a child, "Martin, what were you trying to show us when you held your hands this way (or when you pointed to the map or when you gestured toward Tom)?" Ask the class: "What message did Martin send us with his hands? What advantage was there in using gestures as Martin did? Similarly, as an aside to ongoing class discussion, focus on your own nonverbal clues, "Why do you think I am pointing here?" or "What do I mean when I wave my hands in this way?" or "When we arrange chairs in this pattern, what does it mean we will be doing?" The opportunity for this kind of consideration of nonverbal communication is almost always available.

Of course, too, a visiting classroom speaker provides an opportunity to drive home the importance of nonverbal clues. After the speaker has departed, youngsters can quickly list on charting paper the kinds of gestures, facial expressions, and large-scale motions he used to communicate. They can go on to evaluate whether the speaker used body language effectively, whether his face was expressive, whether he spoke with his eyes, and whether his body was too active or too passive.

Activities such as these need not be divorced from consideration of verbal aspects of communication. Analysis can focus simultaneously on both words and nonverbal clues. In this way, children begin to appreciate nonverbal expression as part of the total communication process. This is vital today when children and adults are receiving more and more of their information and impressions from spoken rather than written language. The need for learning the nonverbal as well as the verbal dimensions of speech is obvious.

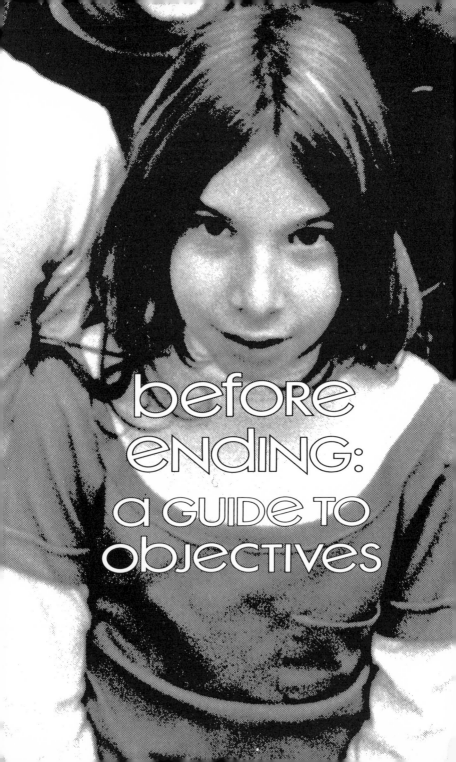

before
ending:
a guide to
objectives

How do we teach children to communicate nonverbally and to become aware of the power of nonverbal language?

To teach nonverbal language skills and awareness, we must provide numerous opportunities that invite nonverbal expression. Teachers can do this when they include discussion, storytelling, pantomiming, dramatic, and listening activities in the curriculum; they do this when they ask youngsters to show as well as tell and to observe the use of nonverbal language in everyday interaction. Obviously such experiences with nonverbal language cannot be separated from the total language program; teaching nonverbal language is a continuous process intimately related to teaching verbal expression.

Through encounters that trigger nonverbal expression and observations of nonverbal interaction, students gradually acquire specific nonverbal language skills and awareness. Just as youngsters gain such verbal skills as the ability to distinguish certain vowel sounds or to distinguish figurative from literal uses of verbal language, so they can gain skills essential for effective nonverbal communication. Nonverbal language skills in youngsters include the physical expressive skills, vocal expressive skills, and interpretation skills identified in the following listings:

PHYSICAL EXPRESSIVE SKILLS
- Using gestures of hands, arms, fingers, feet, head, body, and legs to make verbal messages more clear or emphatic and to take the place of verbal messages where appropriate.
- Controlling the messages one sends through facial expressions so that one sends the messages one intends.

- Varying nonverbal expressions to achieve special effects.
- Relating the speed of gestures and gross body movements to the substance of the messages one is sending.
- Using the entire body at times to communicate meanings, to gain attention of listeners, and to add variety.
- Being aware of the messages one is sending through posture or body stance; using posture deliberately to send messages when necessary.
- Using eyes effectively to convey cognitive meanings, to convey feelings, and to regulate conversational interaction.
- Being aware of the messages one is sending through physical distance, touch, and time; using distance, touch, and time deliberately as part of a message where appropriate.
- Being aware of the messages one is sending through appearance and setting; using appearance and setting as part of the message when appropriate.
- Using complete motionlessness of the body as part of the message.
- Controlling nervous mannerisms manifested in the form of gestures, facial expressions, or gross body movements.

VOCAL EXPRESSIVE SKILLS

- Changing tone of voice to reflect the substance of one's message; using vocal tone to communicate approval/disapproval, concern/lack of concern, or pleasure/fear.
- Varying pitch of voice to show feelings, to emphasize, and to increase the interest level of a listener.
- Controlling loudness of voice depending on the distance between oneself and his listeners.
- Varying loudness of voice to achieve a particular effect, e.g., to startle, to emphasize, or to relay a specific emotional content.

- Using pause effectively as a communication device.
- Speaking at a rate that is compatible with the message being sent.

INTERPRETATION SKILLS
- Interpreting nonverbal messages within the context in which messages are sent.
- Reading gestures as well as gross body motions.
- Reading facial expressions that accompany verbal messages or stand alone as an element of communication.
- Interpreting messages sent through expressions of and contact with the eyes.
- Interpreting messages sent through a person's manipulation of time and space.
- Interpreting messages sent through a person's manipulation of people and objects in a situation.
- Interpreting physical contact as part of a message.
- Perceiving actual meanings beneath the façades people maintain.
- Perceiving subtle nonverbal clues: slight movements of shoulders, shifts of the eyes, or slight changes in facial expression.
- Sifting out mannerisms from a person's other nonverbal actions.
- Identifying one's own hang-ups that determine how one perceives the messages others send.

These expressive and interpretation skills can serve as a checklist for the teacher who wants to build a nonverbal language development program geared to individual differences. Teaching nonverbal language is a type of pioneer enterprise; there are no textbook series available to guide the teacher. The teacher interested in nonverbal language development must define his own program objectives. To do this, he may draw from the above skills checklists.

In implementing an individualized nonverbal language program, the teacher must also diagnose youngsters' individual progress toward program objectives and design further activities to meet individual needs. Again, the checklists can be helpful. They make explicit specific behaviors to be sought, and serve as a framework for diagnosing general weaknesses to be attacked through a total class activity or individual problems to be attacked through a one-to-one or small group activity.

Overemphasis on specific behaviors to be sought, however, has pitfalls. Language lessons that focus on one or two skills can be restricting; the larger goals of instruction, the fun of just playing with language in a creative way, and the opportunities to pursue language experiences that emerge spontaneously will be lost.

To design an activity around one or two skills that are to be measured in rather precise terms at the end of an experience is even more limiting. First, an activity can produce a variety of unanticipated learnings—learnings that may be even more significant than any predefined objectives. Second, many language goals are elusive; many encounters that invite language expression or interpretation are required to reach specific goals, and some goals are beyond precise measurement.

For these reasons, specific behavioral objectives have not been listed with the specific activities described in this book, and a more free-wheeling checklist approach has been advocated. It is the author's hope that with such an approach the activities described will not become highly structured, routine drills. It is her hope that the teacher who knows what nonverbal language is all about will involve children and youths in experiences that stimulate creative use of verbal and nonverbal language. It is her hope that expression-filled experiences will become part of the expanding language base from which children go "forth every day" into new language experiences, even as the child in Walt Whitman's "There Was a Child Went Forth" made each object he encountered part of himself—

There was a child went forth every day,
And the first object he look'd upon, that object he
    became,
And that object became part of him for the day or a
    certain part of the day,
Or for many years or stretching cycles of years.

The early lilacs became part of this child,
And grass and white and red morning-glories, and white
    and red clover, and the song of the phoebe-bird, . . .

The blow, the quick loud word, the tight bargain, the
    crafty lure,
The family usages, the language, the company, the
    furniture, the yearning and swelling heart, . . .

The horizon's edge, the flying sea-crow, the fragrance of
    salt marsh and shore mud,
These became part of that child who went forth every
    day, and who now goes, and will always go forth
    every day.

bibliography

NONVERBAL COMMUNICATION

Birdwhistell, Ray L. *Kinesics and Context: Essays on Body Motion Communication.* Philadelphia: University of Pennsylvania Press, 1972. A series of highly readable essays—some new, some from hard-to-obtain publications—on kinesics. Part I provides examples from daily life; Part II has more technical material.

Cunduff, Merlyn. *Kinesics: The Power of Silent Command.* Englewood Cliffs, N.J.: Parker Publishing, 1972. A book for the layman interested in improving nonverbal language skills.

Davitz, Joel. *The Communication of Emotional Meaning.* New York: McGraw-Hill, 1964. A sophisticated analysis and summary of research studies that investigate the nature of meanings conveyed through vocal and physical expression. Davitz's review of the research is highly readable; studies by Dimitrovsky on children's ability to identify emotional meanings expressed nonverbally and by Beldoch on differences in sensitivity to expression of emotional meanings are of special interest to the classroom teacher.

Fast, Julius. *Body Language.* New York: Pocket Books, 1970. A popular book that speaks to the layman in simple language, providing an easily understood overview of the elements of nonverbal communication, including space, distance, eyes, gestures, stance, and facial expression.

Galloway, Charles M. *Teaching Is Communicating: Nonverbal Language in the Classroom.* Washington, D.C.: Association for Student Teaching, 1970. A pamphlet that looks at nonverbal language as it is used in classrooms by teachers and students; most interesting are the examples of nonverbal classroom interaction.

Goffman, Erving. *Presentation of Self in Everyday Life.* Garden City, N.Y.: Doubleday Anchor Books, 1959. A paperback that presents nonverbal expression as a part of the front or facade that people maintain in their interaction with others. Goffman's point that nonverbal language is often used deliberately in communication is worthy of further consideration.

————. *Strategic Interaction.* Philadelphia: University of Pennsylvania Press, 1972. A short book that presents human interaction as a game-like event in which players' moves are dependent on the moves of other players. Stress is on verbal moves, but Goffman's point has implications for nonverbal communication as well.

Grant, Barbara, and Dorothy Hennings. *The Teacher Moves: An Analysis of Nonverbal Activity.* New York: Teachers College Press, 1971. An investigation of the teacher's use of body language. Part I reports on a study of body language that uses a case study approach; Part II analyzes facets of teachers' nonverbal style; the appendix includes an analysis guide though which a teacher can consider his own nonverbal style.

Hall, Edward T. *The Hidden Dimension.* Garden City, N.Y.: Doubleday, 1966. A landmark investigation of the meanings sent through the manipulation of distance and of the ways people from varying cultures view distance in human encounters.

————. *The Silent Language.* Garden City, N.Y.: Doubleday, 1959. An investigation of time as a communication agent. Hall also considers distance and stresses cultural variations in meanings assigned to time and distance.

Montague, Ashley. *Touching: The Human Significance of the Skin.* New York: Columbia University Press, 1971. An exploration of the messages sent through touch and meanings associated with touch in different cultures.

Scheflen, Albert E. with Alice Schflen. *Body Language and the Social Order.* Englewood Cliffs, N.J.: Prentice-Hall, 1972. An illustrated volume in which Scheflen explains his research findings into nonverbal communication and reveals the ways nonverbal signals can be used to dominate and control others. Consideration is given to decor, facial expressions, and use of uniforms as means of social control.

Sommer, Robert. *Personal Space: The Behavioral Basis of Design.* Englewood Cliffs, N.J.: Prentice-Hall, 1969. An analysis and summary of man's use of space in small groups, institutions, and schools. Particularly interesting are sections related to arrangement of furnishings and to the messages we send through the seating arrangement we select.

Thompson, James. *Beyond Words: Nonverbal Communication in the Classroom.* New York: Citation Press, 1973. An analysis of nonverbal communication designed to help the classroom teacher understand and use nonverbal communication more effectively.

SPECIFIC IDEAS FOR MOVEMENT ACTIVITY, DRAMATIZATIONS, AND PANTOMIMES

Andrews, Gladys. *Creative Rhythmic Movement for Children.* Englewood Cliffs, N.J.: Prentice-Hall, 1954. Ideas to encourage children to create their own patterns of movement and dance—to bounce, to gallop, to run and leap like a deer, to be a top; musical selections that can stimulate skipping, rowing, tugging, mosquitoing, and tick-tocking are included in the text.

Ashton, Dudley. *Rhythmic Activities, Grades K-6.* Washington, D.C.: American Association for Health, Physical

Education and Recreation, n.d. More movement activities that involve youngsters in walking, leaping, skipping, sliding, galloping.

Blackie, Pamela, Bess Bullough, and Doris Nash. *Drama.* New York: Citation Press, 1972. Discussions of drama in the British infant and junior schools. Three teachers discuss basic and expressive movement with specific examples on how to introduce movement, how to involve children in physical characterization, and how to relate movement to feelings to be expressed.

Bentley, William G. *Learning to Move and Moving to Learn.* New York: Citation Press, 1970. Activities to "improve children's skills in body management" as a complement to existing physical education experiences.

Chambers, Dewey. *Storytelling and Creative Drama.* Dubuque, Iowa: Wm. C. Brown, 1970. Ideas for storytelling that apply as much to the teacher storyteller as to the child storyteller and for creative drama, giving a step-by-step account of how to involve youngsters in creative drama.

Cole, Ann, Carolyn Hass, and Faith Bushnell. *I Saw a Purple Cow and 100 Other Recipes for Learning.* Boston: Little, Brown, 1972. Activities for teachers and mothers to use with preschoolers. Some of the "recipes" are for finger plays, riddle contests, and pantomimes that will bring children into direct contact with nonverbal expression.

Fitzgerald, Burdette. *Let's Act the Story.* San Francisco: Fearon, 1957. A teacher reference that gives specific suggestions, in the context of model stories, to help a teacher lead a group in acting out a story.

Latchaw, Marjorie E. *Pocket Guide of Games and Rhythms for the Elementary School.* Englewood Cliffs, N.J.: Prentice-Hall, 1956. Three hundred sixteen pages of rhythm and game activities for use at various grade levels.

Mulac, Margaret. *Games and Stunts for Schools, Camps, and Playgrounds.* New York: Harper & Row, 1964. Useful ideas for involving youngsters in both verbal and nonverbal expression.

Pflug, Elizabeth. *Funny Bags.* Princeton, N.J.: Van Nostrand, 1968. All sorts of ideas for converting a large bottomed bag from the grocery into a mask or puppet for use in dramatizations.

Stuart, Frances, V. L. Gibson, and A. A. Jervey. *Rhythmic Activities,* Series I and II. Minneapolis: Burgess Publishing Co., 1963. A card file of ideas for rhythmic activities.

Taylor, Loren. *Informal Dramatics for Young Children.* Minneapolis: Burgess Publishing, 1965. One of a series which contains specific ideas for rhythmic play, dramatic games, and dramatic play. Other relevant titles in the series include *Pantomime and Pantomime Games, Choral Drama, Radio Drama, Storytelling and Dramatization,* and *Informal Dramatics for Young Children.*

MATERIALS TO USE WITH CHILDREN AND YOUTH

PICTURE SERIES AND CURRICULUM PROGRAMS

Amazing Life Games Theater. Boston: Houghton Mifflin. A package of materials including five films, one of which, *That's Me,* offers children the opportunity to play out their own interpretations of the story. A second introduces children to gestures as part of communication (*Words, Words, Words*); a third (*Little Big Top*) stimulates children to become a "parade of shapes" or the ringmaster of the circus. The package also includes a file of highly innovative teaching suggestions and a box filled with ready-to-use materials that children can work with. Teaching suggestions in the communication skills section are oriented toward the nonverbal.

Discussion Pictures for Beginning Social Studies. New York: Harper & Row, 1967. Sharp, clear, and colored or black-and-white pictures that are just great for interpretation of nonverbal expressions. Organized around personal-social themes such as man's search for security and man's need for association and expression in groups. Can be used through grade four.

Human Value Series—Teaching Pictures. Austin, Tex.: Steck Vaughn. Large-sized colored pictures that depict emotion-charged situations involving youngsters grades two through four. Situations range from the child left out of a dramatic activity to a child taunted by others. Pictures are on heavy cardboard and can stand up with the use of a special mounting attached to the reverse side. Children can interpret the situations or role play what is happening.

Images of Man. New York: Scholastic Magazines, Inc. A program of photographs, sound-slide lectures, and filmstrips that explores some of "the most important human events of the last decades." This material can be used with junior high school students.

Interaction of Man and Man: Paired Inquiry Pictures. Chicago: Rand McNally and Company. More pictures to be used for interpretation of nonverbal expression; close-ups of both interaction between individuals and interaction within crowds. The series can be used with primary school youngsters to stimulate thought and talk about the distances people tend to keep between themselves and others.

Kindle Filmstrips: Who Am I? How Do I Learn? Getting Along? New York: Scholastic Magazines, Inc. Three filmstrip and record/cassette series through which children can encounter feelings about themselves and others. The filmstrips *All Kinds of Feelings, The Joy of Being You,* and *Smiles Don't Just Happen* can be used with primary school children to interpret body expression.

Man and Communities: Concepts and Values. Grand Rapids, Mich.: The Fideler Company. A series of full-color, large-sized pictures organized around themes such as families, families around the world, and the needs of man. Some can be used as material for interpreting facial expressions and body expressions. Middle elementary grades.

Nonverbal Communication: Resources for Teachers. Skokie, Ill.: National Textbook Company. A resource unit containing an explanatory text and specially prepared visuals and activities for use in making nonverbal communication an integral part of communication study. Designed for use in high school, it may be adapted for upper-elementary grades.

People in Action Series: Role-playing and Discussion Photographs for Elementary Social Studies. New York: Holt, Rinehart and Winston. A series of flip-back, spiral bound, black and white photographs that depict children in emotional or action-filled situations. Facial expressions are particularly clear. Pictures are in levels: A, B, C, etc., with lower levels being more appropriate for use with younger elementary children. A teachers' guide accompanies each level to help the teacher who wants to use the pictures to stimulate role playing.

Schools, Families, Neighborhoods: A Multi-media Readiness Program. Chicago: Field Educational Publications. A box of pictures and filmstrips depicting neighborhoods and schools. Some can be used to stimulate discussion and/or role playing in middle-elementary grades. Records go with the package.

Who Am I? New York: William H. Sodlier, Inc. A box of materials some of which can be used for stimulating dramatic activity in K-1. Includes a teachers' manual of ideas, murals that can be used as a background for dramatization, some "costumes" (picture sheets that a player can hold in front of himself) as well as a rather good record.

You and Me. Lexington, Mass.: Ginn and Co. Clear, large, and black, blue or green and white study prints. Organized around themes such as interacting with others and understanding needs for social control, the prints are excellent for interpreting nonverbal communication.

FILMS

Chairy Tale. Ten minutes, black and white, International Film Bureau. A pantomime of a man struggling against a chair that has a will of its own. After viewing the film, youngsters can pantomime their own struggles with an unwieldy hammer or with a sticky door.

Chinese Shadow Play. Ten minutes, color, Contemporary Films. The legend of "The White Snake Lady" told with rod puppets that perform behind an illuminated screen. After viewing the film, youngsters can make their own rod puppets and create a shadow play based on a folk tale.

Christmas Cracker. Nine minutes, color, Contemporary Films. A jester in costume introduces three acts; in one boy and girl paper cut-outs move to "Jingle Bells." Youngsters can make similar paper cut-outs to move to other snappy tunes.

Dance Your Own Way. Eleven minutes, color, University of California. A bright, lively film in which children clap hands to the rhythm of music and then skip, sway, stamp, and turn to the rhythm. During a second run-through youngsters can participate in the film action

The Doughnuts. Twenty-six minutes, color, Weston Woods. A live-action dramatization of the doughnut episode from Robert McCloskey's *Homer Price.* The film can be used to motivate groups to dramatize episodes from other books children are reading.

Harold and the Purple Crayon. Ten minutes, color, Brandon. A drawing story in which Harold draws a wood, trees, a picnic lunch, and finally his very own bed. Use this film with books like *The Tale of a Black Cat* to get children involved in concocting their own drawing stories. Related books are Zinken Hopp's *Magic Chalk* (McKay) and Douglas and Elizabeth MacAgy's *Going for a Walk with a Line* (Doubleday). Weston Woods has an animated version of the same story.

Island of the Blue Dolphins. Ninety-three minutes, color, United World Films (rental only). Scott O'Dell's Newbery Award-winning story of an Indian girl separated from her tribe. The film can stimulate group dramatic activities that draw their storyline from a book.

Kumak, the Sleepy Hunter. Thirteen minutes, color, Radim. The tale of a sleepy hunter told through puppets. The film can trigger storytelling with puppets.

Little Blue and Little Yellow. Nine minutes, color, Contemporary Films. An animated version of Leo Lionni's great little book. The film can be a springboard into storytelling with a flannel board.

The Little Mariner. Twenty minutes, color, Encyclopedia

Britannica Films. The tale of a small boy in an en-
chanted sailboat told completely without words. The
film can spark activity in which youngsters tell tales
without a narration.

Mr. Koumal. Each vignette, 1½–2½ minutes, color,
Weston Woods. A series of animated, nonverbal vi-
gnettes for use in junior high school classes. Each vignette illustrates some of the ironies and predicaments
of life. Titles in the series include: *Mr. Koumal Carries
the Torch, Mr. Koumal Moves to the Country, Mr. Koumal Discovers Koumalia,* and *Mr. Koumal Gets Involved.*

Niok. Twenty-nine minutes, color, Walt Disney. The
story of Ayot's search for his lost elephant friend. Told
through photography and with limited narration, the
film is especially useful in stimulating talk about nonverbal ways we learn about what is going on.

A Scrap of Paper and a Piece of String. Six minutes,
color, Contemporary Films. An animated film about the
antics of a scrap of paper and a piece of string. Ask
children who see the film to devise other ways of telling the story—puppets, flannel board, and live action.

The Steadfast Tin Soldier. Fourteen minutes, color, Brandon. Another animated film telling the well-known Andersen tale. Use it with the book, *The Steadfast Tin
Soldier,* illustrated by Marcia Brown (Scribners, 1953)
to motivate a Hans Christian Andersen Extravaganza.

The Stone Cutter. Six minutes, color, International Film
Foundation. The tale of the impoverished stone cutter
told through paper cut-outs. It can be an introduction
to storytelling with flannel board.

Stone Soup. Eleven minutes, color, Weston Woods. The
classic folk tale of the people who were gullible enough

to believe they could make soup from stones. An icono-
graphic film like many of the Weston Woods films,
Stone Soup can motivate children to dramatize stories
taken from books.

The Tale of Custard the Dragon. Six minutes, color,
Weston Woods. A live action film useful to motivate
dramatic interpretation of stories.

WRITTEN MATERIALS

Burroughs, Margaret T. *Did You Feed My Cow?* Chicago:
Follett, 1969. Street games, chants, and rhymes, many
of which can involve youngsters of elementary age
with movement expression.

Carlson, Bernice. *Listen! And Help Tell the Story.* Nash-
ville, Tenn.: Abingdon Press, 1965. Finger plays (or
handies), action verses, poems for body chants, and
stories with sound effects for youngsters in grades two
through four.

Cullum, Albert. *Aesop in the Afternooon.* New York:
Citation Press, 1972. Sixty-six playlets from the fables
of Aesop for use in grades two through five. Youngsters
can read the fables written in play form and then improvise their own words and actions.
———. *Greek Tears and Roman Laughter: Ten Tragedies and Five Comedies for Schools.* New York: Citation
Press, 1970. Adaptations of five Greek tragedies and
ten Roman comedies for children in upper-elementary
and junior high. Youngsters can use the scripts supplied by Cullum or improvise their own after a rapid
reading of the plays.

Emberley, Ed. *Punch and Judy: A Play for Puppets.*
Boston: Little, Brown, 1965. The tragic comedy presented in a form for easy interpretation through pup-
petry.

Gaeddert, Lou Ann, illustrated by Gioia Fiammenghi. *Noisy Nancy Norris.* Garden City, N.Y.: Doubleday, 1965. The story of Nancy who bangs her feet, thumps her clay, sounds a fireman's siren, and bangs pans together. Because of the noisy accompaniment, it is great for telling. In the Scott, Foresman Talking Storybook Series the book is accompanied by a record.

Glass, Paul. *Songs and Stories of the North American Indians.* New York: Grosset and Dunlap, 1968. Stories and songs of the Pawnee, the Papago, the Teton Sioux, the Yuma, and the Mandan. Older elementary youngsters can use the book to build dramatic musical sequences about Indian life.

————. *Songs and Stories of Afro-Americans.* New York: Grosset and Dunlap, 1971. Stories of songs that evidence the rich cultural heritage of the Afro-American. Older youngsters can use the book to build dramatic musical sequences about the life of Afro-Americans.

Gould, Carmen and Louise Ely. *Showtime with Hoky Horse.* New York: Holt, Rinehart and Winston, 1964. For children in grades two through four showing how to make a horse from a paper bag, a blanket, and a broom. It gives ideas on how children can put together a circus act.

Hazen, Barbara Shook. *Happy, Sad, Silly, Mad.* New York: Wonder Books, 1971. A little book that explores the way we feel when we feel happy, sad, silly, or mad. It can be used as a jump-off into nonverbal expression of those emotions with young children.

Hurd, Michael. *Sailor's Songs and Shanties.* New York: Henry Walck, 1965. Supplies explanations of sailors' songs as well as the songs themselves. Youngsters who want to do sailor skits can learn the songs, make tapes of their renditions, and use the tapes as musical background. Appropriate for upper grades.

Max, Peter. *The Land of Yellow; The Land of Red; The Land of Blue.* New York: all Franklin Watts, 1970. Way-out books that can stimulate youngsters to put together wild dramatic sequences juxtaposed against one another. In the books, colors blare at the reader, and sounds like zappy, zowie, and wowie shreak; the result is a psychedelic trip that can trigger creative thinking.

McGee, Barbara. *Jump Rope Rhymes.* New York: Viking, 1968. Poems—often of a nonsensical nature—to which youngsters can jump or which can be converted into body chants.

O'Neill, Mary. *Words, Words, Words.* Garden City, N.Y.: Doubleday, 1966. Poems such as "Moon," Happiness Has Five Children," "Sloopy," and "Felicity" that can be used as a discussion springboard about how we interpret nonverbal signals like "dirty necks," "untied shoes," and "tone of voice."

Sanders, Sandra. *Creating Plays with Children.* New York: Citation Press, 1970. A handbook to guide the elementary teacher working with children who are creating their own plays. Five plays by children are included.

Segal, Edith. *Come with Me.* New York: Citadel Press, 1963, pp. 49-62. A series of poems that can be interpreted through movement; others work well as body chants.

Temko, Florence, and Elaine Simon. *Paper Folding to Begin With.* Indianapolis: Bobbs-Merrill, 1968. Shows how to make birds, pigs, cats, dogs and the like by folding paper; the heads that are formed can be used as hand puppets for improvised dramatics.

Worstell, Emma. *Jump the Rope Jingles.* New York: Macmillan, 1961. Traditional jump rope jingles, many of which can be converted to body chants.

RECORDINGS—RHYTHM RECORDS

Activity Songs for Kids. Scholastic Audio-Visual Materials, Englewood Cliffs, N.J. Songs about children's special experiences with the world around them. The songs encourage children to sing along and act out the situations embodied in the folk tunes.

Adventures in Rhythm; Call and Response Rhythmic Group Singing; This Is Rhythm. Scholastic Audio-Visual Materials, Englewood Cliffis, N.J. A series of recordings that invite children to participate in the sounds and in the motions. Features Ella Jenkins.

Dance A Story Series. RCA Records, Educational Sales, P.O. Box RCA 1000, Indianapolis, Ind. A series of records that entice children to "Dance a Story about Little Duck," "Dance a Story—Balloons," and "Dance a Story—The Magic Mountain." In response to the records, young children concoct nonverbal stories.

Counting Games and Rhythms for the Little Ones. Scholastic Audio-Visual Materials, Englewood Cliffs, N.J. Just what the title suggests—a way of getting young children involved in rhythmic expression.

Sing 'n Do Albums. Sing 'n Do Company, Midland Park, N.J. These recordings easily encourage dramatization, pantomiming, and singing-action sequences. Note particularly Album #1 (Grades K–3) in which musical selections stimulate children to "become" trains, to gesture, to "become" puppets, and to march; in Album #2 (Grades K-3) selections stimulate children to "become" a hen, to simulate wind action, to jump and so forth.

RECORDINGS—STORIES

Caedmon Records, 505 Eighth Avenue, New York, N.Y., has a fine selection of records and tape cassettes of children's stories that can provide the content of dramatization and pantomime as well as material that children can listen to and then share verbally and non-verbally in storytelling. Some excellent recordings to use in this way include:

Happy Birthday to You! and Other Stories. Some Dr. Seuss favorites read by Hans Conried.

The Emperor's New Clothes and Other Tales by Hans Christian Andersen. Michael Redgrave reading "The Tinder Box, "The Emperor's Nightingale," and other Andersen favorites.

Just So Stories. Boris Karloff reading some of the tales from Rudyard Kipling's *The Jungle Book.*

The Tale of Peter Rabbit and Other Stories. Some of Beatrix Potter read by Claire Bloom.

American Tall Tales, volumes 1, 2, 3, and 4. Ed Begley reading such old time favorites as Davy Crockett, Pecos Bill, Johnny Appleseed, Paul Bunyan and John Henry.

Miller-Brody Productions, 342 Madison Avenue, New York, N.Y., has a number of excellent recordings of "talking books"—readings of short stories and juvenile favorites by great voices of the theater. Recordings youngsters can hear in listening stations and then re-tell through dramatization and pantomime include:

Adventures of Pinocchio. The long-nosed favorite.

Arabian Nights. A rendition including "Aladdin," "Sin-bad," and "Ali Baba."

Grimm's Fairy Tales. Old time favorites such as "Hansel and Gretel," "The Gallant Tailor," and "Rumpelstil-skin."

In addition, Miller-Brody is now making available re-cordings of Newbery Award winning books such as *From the Mixed-up Files of Mrs. Basil E. Frankweiler, Caddie Woollawn* and *Amos Fortune, Free Man.* This material again can be a source of stories to tell or to dramatize.

Scholastic Audio-Visual Materials, Englewood Cliffs, N.J., has available a record-book companion series that youngsters can listen to and read. Stories in the series include: *City Mouse—Country Mouse and Two More Mouse Tales from Aesop, Curious George Rides a Bike, Bread and Jam for Frances,* and *Lentil.*

Spoken Arts, Inc., 310 North Avenue, New Rochelle, N.Y., has a large selection of materials available on cassettes: fairy tales, fables, poems, stories, and tales from other lands. Children can listen to and then dramatize the tales and stories for their classmates. Spoken Arts also has a selection of taped dramatizations that includes such favorites as: *The Monkey's Paw, Hans Brinker, The King of the Golden River,* and *Rapunzel.* Tall tales, fables, myths, legends, folk tales are available on records.

Weston Woods, Weston, Conn., continues to supply records and cassettes of children's stories. There is a vast listing of such goodies as: *Where the Wild Things Are, Whistle for Willie, Tikki Tikki Tembo, Rosie's Walk, Frog Went A-Courtin',* and *Chanticleer and the Fox.* This material can be made available to youngsters in listening stations for individual and group listening; youngsters who have listened to the same recording can form groups for dramatic sharing of the stories with children who have not heard the story.